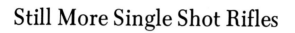

Still More Single Shot Rifles

Still More Single Shot Rifles

by
JAMES J. GRANT

Pioneer Press
Union City, Tennessee   1979

STILL MORE SINGLE SHOT RIFLES

CONTENTS

VOLUME IV—Still More Single Shot Rifles

Plate Number 1 Stevens Favorite in Original Box
Plate Number 2 Stevens Favorite Box
Plate Number 3 Cased Stevens Favorite Side Plate Rifle
Plate Number 4 Stevens Wind Gauge Front Sight
Plate Number 5 An odd sized Tip-up Stevens Frame (2 Prints this plate)
Plate Number 6 Stevens Side Plate
Plate Number 7 Stevens Small Frame Side Plate Rifle
Plate Number 8 Stevens Side Plate Rifles
Plate Number 9 Stevens Side Plate Rifle
Plate Number 10 Stevens Bisley Model Rifle
Plate Number 11 Stevens Bisley Model Frame Marking
Plate Number 12 Stevens Model 46-44
Plate Number 13 Stevens Model 47-44
Plate Number 14 Stevens Rifle Model No. 109 W/2 Barrels
Plate Number 15 Stevens Rifle Model 50-44
Plate Number 16 Left Side Rifle Model 50-44
Plate Number 17 Right Side Rifle Model 50-44
Plate Number 18 Stevens Special Pope Model Rifle
Plate Number 19 Stevens Model 044½ Special Order Rifle
Plate Number 20 Stevens Model 110 Rifle
Plate Number 20A Stevens-Pope Model 44½
Plate Number 21 A. A. Clive Patent
Plate Number 22 A. A. Clive Patent
Plate Number 23 A. A. Clive Patent
Plate Number 24 A. A. Clive Patent
Plate Number 25 A. A. Clive Rifle Action Opened
Plate Number 26 A. A. Clive Rifle Action Dissassembled
Plate Number 27 G. P. Gunn Patent
Plate Number 28 G. P. Gunn Patent Text
Plate Number 29 G. P. Gunn Patent Text
Plate Number 30 Meriden Model 6 Rifle
Plate Number 31 Meriden Model 6 Barrel Marking
Plate Number 32 Empire State Cadet Rifle
Plate Number 33 Empire State Cadet Rifle Action Open
Plate Number 34 Empire State Cadet Rifle Lever & Block Removed
Plate Number 35 Empire State Cadet Breech Mechanism
Plate Number 36 Belgian Flobert With Double Set Triggers
Plate Number 37 Trigger Plate Dismounted from Flobert Rifle
Plate Number 38 The Opened Breech of Rifle Shown on Plate Number 36
Plate Number 39 A Hammerless Flobert Specimen
Plate Number 40 Circular of the Japanese Hamilton Model 27
Plate Number 40A The Japanese Hamilton Rifle
Plate Number 41 Japanese Bolt Action Rifle
Plate Number 42 The Ross .22 Caliber Rifle (2 Prints)
Plate Number 43 The "Bull Frog Sr." Rifle
Plate Number 44 The "Wild Cat" Rifle
Plate Number 45 Hang Tag from the "Wildcat" Rifle
Plate Number 46 Hopkins & Allen Catalogue Insert Sheet
Plate Number 47 Reverse of Sheet Shown on Plate Number 46
Plate Number 48 1915 Catalogue of Iver Johnson Sporting Goods Company
Plate Number 49 From the 1915 Catalogue of Iver Johnson Sporting Goods
    Company
Plate Number 50 Hopkins & Allen Bicycle Rifle
Plate Number 51 Hopkins & Allen Bicycle Rifle Action Opened

Preface

This is difficult! Difficult in the sense that I must proceed with another book on single shot rifles. Especially since in the introduction to *Volume Three Boys' Single Shot Rifles,* I mentioned that that one might be the last of the series.

When that introduction was written I did not plan another book; in fact, had no idea such a thing could be possible. However, in order to expedite that volume some later data was withheld to speed up the publishing of the book. Production was delayed, however, and in the rush to get the book published by deadline, the photo credits were left off each individual plate and had to be listed on a page in the front of the book. And, at that, some of them were credited incorrectly. I want to take this opportunity to apologize to those contributors of photographs which appeared in *Boys' Single Shot Rifles.*

I still feel, too, the choice of a title for *Volume Three* was unfortunate. Being called a boys' rifle book deterred many from buying it, some waited too long, and still others learned too late only half covered the light boys' type pieces while the balance of the book contained additional material on the heavy target and sporting rifles previously covered in the first two books.

I have always been sorry the book was not named "Still More Single Shot Rifles," partly because it contained illustrations and data on some beautiful and rare serious target pieces. Many times I wondered how the owners of some of these rifles would feel about having their property included in a book called "Boys' Rifles." If any men have felt offended or slighted in any degree by this, they have not communicated their feelings on it to me and for this I am grateful.

It is my hope and plan that this volume be called *'Still More Single Shot Rifles'* since we missed using this title for *Volume Three.* To add the additional material to revised editions of previous books has not been my policy. Why should the reader be forced to buy again the material already covered by previous books? Instead I believe this new material can be covered better with an entirely new volume.

After all, none of the preceding data is dated in any way, it doesn't go out of style and as I have mentioned many times, the story of single shot rifles is a continuing story. Remarks such as this are the only reading matter you are forced to buy again.

There are some lighter type of boys' rifles included herein but I am sure the collectors of these will not feel overlooked by using the above title. In the over thirty years that have elapsed since the publishing of *Volume One* in 1947, I have noted a gradual change in the collecting field, at least in the field of single shots. There are many more interested now than when I started collecting. At that time there were few of us and I knew most of them, either personally or through correspondence.

After the Ohio Gun Collectors Association was formed in the mid-thirties, there were only two or three single shot collectors who attended the Ohio gun shows. If one of us did not buy the few pieces offered they went begging. At that time the association consisted mainly of serious collectors of various types of arms. There were almost no dealers in evidence, though little by little, more and more dealers became members.

The best definition of a collector versus a dealer was given by the late Jim White of Illinois when he said, "a dealer carries his purchase openly into the house, while a collector generally smuggles his in!"

One of the puzzling changes, at least to me, is the fact present day collectors must have only single shot rifles which are in factory new condition, or as some call it 'mint condition.' To me, this is a term which has no value whatever in the precise descriptions of a collector's arm. Being somewhat of an old fogey, I believe the standard NRA terms are much more valuable than any others in present use. After viewing many rifles at many gun shows the past years, I am of the opinion, most, not all of course, of the 'collectors' are not collectors at all, they are merely accumulators. I agree that good, clean original rifles are very scarce today. I look them over and most have some detail that is not right. Wrong sights, or no sights at all, incorrect wood or lever, etc. Some are offered as 'mint' which have a fairly good outside appearance and a very rough bore. It is a fact that a few models are very scarce, mostly plainer hunting models, and are rare in new condition. They are rare in any condition, yet some will pass them up if ever offered because they do not realize their scarcity and are blinded by the poor appearance of the piece. That is one reason I call some of them accumulators instead of collectors.

Another facet of the present day collectors' field which baffles me is the lack of interest in the caliber of the piece and in using the thing for the purpose for which it was made, that is shooting. When I collected, I shot them all. Part of the pleasure of obtaining and owning the rifles was getting the correct tools, moulds, cartridges and cases, and using them to ascertain what they would do at the target range.

When I disposed of my rifle collection, I was dumbfounded to learn most buyers weren't the slightest bit interested in also getting the correct tool, mould, cases, etc. to go with the rifle. I disposed of most of these accessories separately later. Some rifle collectors do also collect tools and moulds as well, mainly with the idea of showing these with the pieces themselves, not with the idea of shooting the rifle. There are also people who collect only loading tools and, etc., as well as those who only collect cartridges. I am certainly not attacking these hobbies as I understand the collecting urge—I've had it for years. I just want to make the point that I personally was, and am, interested in the whole thing . . . the rifle, its sights, its ammunition, making that ammunition and using the complete assembly to punch holes in paper targets, since the bison and elk have gotten rather scarce in these parts. I formerly hunted small game, woodchucks, etc., but gave that up too. Hunting these varmints is fun but doesn't offer much shooting and I like to shoot. That is why I would instead take two or three rifles to the range where I could while away a few hours firing possibly one or two hundred experimental rounds.

Then there is also the true collector, who loves the rifles, likes to shoot and yearns for more and more in print concerning his favorite hobby. That is the reason for these books and it has been a great gratification sharing my pleasures in this field with this sort of collector.

With prices of good rifles being what they are today, most who are interested must satisfy themselves with just a few good pieces instead of a large collection. It is a far cry from the days when I gathered together a complete collection of American single shot rifles. Then it was possible for a person of very modest means to get them together without going hungry as well. They weren't nearly so well appreciated in those days and so were priced accordingly.

To sum up, here is 'Still More Single Shot Rifles' and I hope it will help. I have stated in the past, perhaps several times, I hope it is not the last work that will ever be written by me or by anyone.

STILL MORE SINGLE SHOT RIFLES

I

Stevens

To resume the Steven's story continued from *'Boys' Single Shot Rifles,'* some of the following remarks and rifles pictured were received too late to be included in that book.

In *Boys' Rifles* I mentioned I was not sure about the correct name of the smaller frame Model 1885 or "side plate" rifle. I said it was the approximate size frame of the later Favorites but had no idea if it was also called Favorite. However, it *was* called Favorite we now know, as one of these early pieces has turned up in its original factory box.

On *Plate Number 1* this rifle is illustrated contained in its factory box. The rifle is serial numbered 2562.

Plate Number 2 shows the end of the box cover with its label. This label is printed on pale yellow paper with black lettering proclaiming it to be, in fact, a Favorite. The small lettering printed on the lower left corner of this label also contains a date of 1892. So there you have it straight from the old Stevens factory and we can all stop worrying about the name of the early small frame model rifle.

I append herewith all the vital statistics of this interesting find:

Name of Rifle: Stevens Favorite

Model: First Favorite Model, built on the Model 1885 side plate frame.

Maker: J. Stevens Arms & Tool Company

Serial Number: 2562 (Written in chalk on wood under butt plate are last 3 digits of the serial number '562').

Marked on top of the barrel: "J. Stevens A & T Co., Chicopee Falls, Mass. Pat'd. August 11, 1885"

Serial numbers are stamped in front of frame both on the frame and on the side plate. These may be seen when barrel or forend is removed.

1

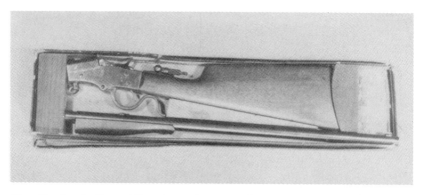

Plate Number 1   Stevens Favorite in the original box. (Photo: Edson Klinkel).

Plate Number 2   Original Stevens Favorite box showing end label.
(Photo: Edson Klinkel).

Action type: Under lever rolling block
Caliber: .22 rimfire
Barrel Length: 36½ inches
Butt Plate: Fairly heavy steel rifle pattern, no lip on top.
Sights: Lyman Ivory Bead front, Lyman two leaf folding rear,
   barrel sight and Lyman folding tang sight with turn down
   peep.
Frame: Frame, lever and butt plate casehardened in colors.
   Hammer, trigger and barrel are blued.
Factory Original: Yes, with possible exception of the Lyman
   sights.
Takedown: Yes, with the ring take-down screw typical of
   Stevens.
   Remarks: Imagine lucking onto a side plate Stevens Favorite in the
original factory box! Well, Ed Klinkel did just that and this is the
rifle. He found it at an Ohio Gun Collectors show in its original
heavy cardboard box. The rifle is in remarkably good condition for a
small .22 rifle; and the box, while it shows wear and tear to a certain
extent, is complete except for one end. It is made of fairly thick

2

cardboard and the outside coating was a black paper layer. The label end of the box is still intact and reads as follows: "STEVENS FAVORITE RIFLE" in large upper case letters. In small thin letters below and to the left side of the label the following appears: "5m 9-92 D.P. Co." These printed letters are in black on a pale yellow paper label pasted to the end of the box cover. Written in pencil at lower right corner of the label is ".22 cal." Now if the small letters mean what we think they do, the box was made, or at least the label was printed, May 9, 1892 by the D. P. Company whoever that might be. If that is so, could this be the first appearance of the side plate Favorite? Or was this just preparation for its announcement in the 1894 catalogue? More than likely the model was announced as early as 1892, possibly earlier.

This frame when disassembled reveals the extractor pivoted upon a screw holding it to the left wall inside the frame. A screw in the top of the breech block leg enables the block-lever assembly to be tightened by backing out this screw. A small screw threaded up into the frame cavity about halfway between the lever fulcrum screw and take down screw may be run in or out to adjust the distance the breech block will drop when lever is opened. It is not long enough to contact the lower face of the block leg when the screw is turned clear in, though, so the purpose of this screw is not clear.

Not to be undone we also submit for your perusal and I hope, approval, a cased model 1885 Favorite. *Plate Number 3* shows this one in its wood coffin. This is also a Favorite in .22 rimfire caliber. I have no idea if the case is Stevens Factory work or not. It is a thin wood case, covered outside in imitation black leather and lined with dark blue velvet or plush. The workmanship displayed in the manufacture of this case is of a high grade, so it is either of Stevens make or some other professional manufactory.

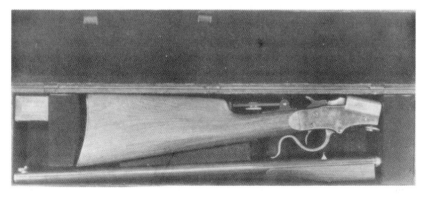

Plate Number 3   Stevens Favorite "Sideplate" Model 1885 in original wooden case. (Photo: Robert Miller, Pittsburgh).

3

I have talked very much about odd items which came from the Stevens works, so by now you may be inclined as I am, to appear very blasé about it all and not show any surprise whatever when confronted with unusual details such as this. The main thing is to not get excited and go all to pieces but just put on a good poker face even though you are seething with excitement inside.

Plate Number 4 illustrates an original, boxed Stevens Wind Gauge front target sight. You will note the label reads 'Manufactured by Stevens.' This brings me back again to the old riddle of just who made the target front sights and vernier tang sights used on various American single shot rifles. There is no doubt the factories had facilities to manufacture their own target sights as well as the common open front and rear barrel patterns. Some have conjectured a private outside company manufactured sights for all the arms companies.

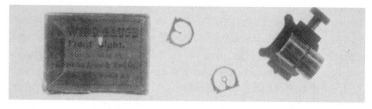

Plate Number 4   Stevens Wind Gauge front sight.

(Photo: Robert Miller, Pittsburgh).

I still feel each factory made the sights for its own use. The pattern varies from rifle to rifle, none are standardized. Since we have discussed the foregoing side plate Favorite rifles, perhaps I should stick with that subject and not go bouncing off in all directions.

Quite a few more 1885 rifles have been brought to my attention lately. One I saw at a small gun show had a serial number of 1204 on the action and lever but the number on the barrel was 255. The owner of the rifle had no idea when the parts were switched and neither have I so mark up a miss for me.

Bill French has a side plate Favorite in .22 rimfire caliber, serial number 21 stamped only on the front of receiver and on the side plate. This specimen has only one screw in the front part of side plate. This is identical to the side plate shown in *More Single Shot Rifles.*

Jay Wilkinson reports seeing and examining a side plate Favorite with a full length forend with two barrel bands in .22 caliber. He stated the forend appears to be original but I make no comment on this as I haven't examined the rifle personally. I have had reports of two other Favorites, the later ones, not the 1885 pattern with full length forends, but remain non-committal on these also.

4

Another side plate Favorite in .22 Long Rifle rimfire is numbered 1745. This number appears on underside of barrel, front face of frame, on front face of side plate and also on several of the action parts. This has a full round 22-inch barrel.

Top of the barrel housing of receiver is the usual round style. This rifle block has a large flat headed screw on that portion which contacts the frame. This is for the purpose of indirectly exerting pressure on the link when the action is closed to keep the lever in a locked-up position. Some have this feature while others lack it.

Now I want to leave the side plate Favorite for a time to discuss some other smaller rifles by Stevens. I will return shortly to talk about some interesting larger side plate jobs and to go into the strange, earlier Ideal or 1894 models.

We've seen another Stevens with a proprietary name on it. It is to all appearances identical with the Model 16 Crackshot Stevens but is marked "Rogers Arms Company Pat. appl. for. .22 Long Rifle." Serial number is A13339. So far I haven't found any data on Rogers Arms Company and probably will not as this may be only the name of a distributor or wholesale hardware company.

I should mention here that variations in Stevens boys' rifles continue to come to light. Some Model 14 Stevens do have butt plates, thin steel ones, in fact. Some also sport the marking "Pat. July 2, 1907."

The Model 26 Crackshot of third variety, the ones with the pistol grip stock and forend, mostly seem to have slightly heavier frames than the usual and more common No. 26 rifles seen. These fall into the Savage Arms category, of course.

The Stevens Maynard Junior rifles have some variations also. The flat board stocks were apparently used on the earliest production examples. This type stock was accompanied by a forend made of similar construction which had a rather blunt tip compared to later issues. The earlier front sight was a half round, while later, they used a rectangular blade. The primary and most marked difference between the two issues is the length of the frame, the earlier frame being approximately 1/8" shorter. Another variation is noted in the later issue. Rivets (two each) were used in lieu of screws at the extreme rear of the frame. These are barely visible to the naked eye. Recently I saw a Favorite, 3rd model, to all appearances, with a seven o'clock extractor. It sported a 5/8" tube Malcolm telescopic sight. Also, believe it or not, a Favorite with a Stevens-Pope light weight .22 long rifle barrel. Serial number was D12. The rifle had mounted on the barrel an L. N. Mogg, Marcellus, N.Y., nickle-plated tube telescopic sight.

Recently a Stevens Model 55, the Ladies Model Rifle on the Favorite action, turned up. This rifle is marked on front of the frame '55.' Serial number is 57043. The slip-in barrel is marked under the forearm wood '.22 7 1/2,' which designated the caliber as .22 WRF. The rifle is mounted with a full length telescopic sight made by R.C. Rice, Warren, Ohio. Rice was listed as an active gunsmith in the city directory of 1899. No notice of him is taken again until, in 1912, his wife is listed as the widow of Raspar C. Rice. I have not, to date, seen another scope by this maker.

Just for variety, let's talk about some Stevens Tip-up pistol grip rifles. You will recall I showed several fine specimens of these in *Boys' Single Shot Rifles*. I recently saw one of these which had had the pistol grip added flatly to the lower part, not channeled for the lower tang of the action. As the stock was uncheckered either at grip or forestock, I assumed this to be an altered-by-gunsmith job. However, Jim Cain has a nice Stevens deluxe pistol grip 1864 Tip-up. Barrel was originally .22 short or long rifle, but had been rechambered for the .22 W.C.F. cartridge in the past. Original barrel length of 29", half round, half octagon. Serial number is 30488 which falls in the serial series I cited in *Boys' Rifles*. The important thing about this piece is that at the point where the lower tang meets the beginning of the pistol grip a slight damage to the wood here brings to light a separation line between the pistol grip and the main body of the buttstock. This indicates that on this rifle, at least, the stock was made in two pieces such as some Maynard stocks. The separation line is only partially evident, however, and the remainder of the continued line is well hidden by the superb woodwork and checkering job done at the Stevens plant when the rifle was made. It is possible then, that when these were made, the wood was first fitted together in two pieces, then finished and checkered as one. The line between the two pieces is hidden (perfectly) by Stevens craftsmanship. In short, this division would not be evident at all on an excellent example of this model, and would lead to the logical conclusion that the stock and pistol grip were of one piece. It is entirely possible some of these deluxe pistol grip stocks were so fabricated in the tip-up, but all I have seen are obviously one piece with the grip channeled to receive the lower tang and the channel carefully and expertly filled with closely matching wood. The cuts to enable the mortising of the lower tang through these grips are detectable by careful observation.

Plate Number 5 illustrates an unusual pistol grip Tip-up Stevens rifle. I bought this rifle some few years back at an Ohio Gun Collectors show. This one is unusual inasmuch as it has an odd sized

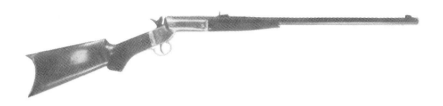

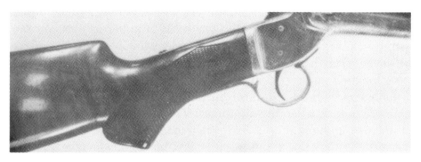

Top: Plate Number 5 Stevens odd-sized frame tip-up pistol grip rifle.
Below: Plate Number 5 Close-up of Stevens tip-up pistol grip rifle.

frame. All pistol gripped models I have seen were on the large sized frame. This seems to be the frame used on the Tip-up shotguns. However, the frame on the rifle illustrated is smaller in size, but not as small as that used on the regular Ladies Model Tip-up rifles. This is a deluxe little rifle in .22 short rimfire caliber. The grip is well checkered, but not in the same pattern as used on the ones shown in *Boys' Rifles.* The pistol grip is built in the usual manner of these pieces, lower tang being fitted through a cut-out section of the wood then the channel refilled. I have not seen another frame this size; however, I do not submit it is the only one in existence, for I am sure Stevens would not have made just one. It's entirely possible others are floating around, perhaps with the usual straight grip style stock?

To thoroughly confuse you, we will look at some more Model 1885 Stevens, but this time the larger sized frame rifles. First of these is a .25 centerfire rifle serial numbered 152, which appears to be one of the earlier ones. This rifle has a slip-in barrel shank, not threaded into the frame. It is held in place by means of the screw upward through the projection on lower front of the frame.

I recently learned about another side plate rifle in .32-40 caliber; but, at this time, haven't been able to verify this nor get further particulars.

Side plate rifle, serial number 76, was listed in the table in *Boys'*
Rifles. I am now able to give more details on that particular gun. It
has the threaded in barrel, caliber .25-20 SS. It is serial numbered on
all parts . . . barrel, extractor, breech block, front of receiver on
both sides of barrel screw boss, lower tang, on lever, and underside
of butt plate. It is unusual to find one so generously endowed, but it
leaves no doubt concerning its originality. There is also a link
adjusting screw in the lever arm of breech block.

The lowest serial number so far encountered on an 1885 model
rifle is 21. This has an intermediate size frame, between the Favorite
and the later model 44 frames. The serial number appears on the
frame at the front on the barrel, on the detachable side plate and on
the lever. The hammer, however, is marked 25, the block and
extractor are numbered 2 and this number also appears on the shank
of the barrel. Perhaps this is the barrel weight designation or possibly
these are shop or assembly numbers?? The barrel is part octagon and
has the slip-in shank, it is 25 5/8" long and is in .25 rimfire caliber.

Another rifle bears serial number 254 on the lower tang, on the
barrel under the forearm, the lever and, on two pieces inside the
action. The buttstock under the butt plate carries this number also.
The 24" part octagon barrel is in .22 Long Rifle caliber. It is
stamped, as are most, 'J. Stevens A & T Co., Chicopee Falls, Mass.
Pat'd. August 11, 1885.'

An anomoly which occurs on most of these side plate action breech
blocks is the transverse blind hole in the lever arm of the block,
halfway between the corner of the 'L' and the pivot screw. This hole
has no obvious function but it possibly may be for a milling jig, etc.?

A late report concerns a Model 1885 rifle with a deluxe pistol grip
stock of burl walnut checkered like the Tip-up pistol grip rifles. This
rifle has the No. 2 Swiss butt plate and is .32-40 caliber. More later
on this one.

My friend, Ed Klinkel, found a frame only from a side plate rifle
at a gun show some time back. The side plate and the lower tang,
which were apparently in one piece, are missing. The frame, or part
of a frame, has no marking or numbers any place and it was
evidently nickle-plated as traces of this are still visible. The barrel
holding screw is in the usual projection of the frame at front and the
extractor is secured to the inner wall of the receiver with a screw
tapped into that wall. So far no trace of the rest of the frame or rifle
have turned up, nor are they likely to do so. See *Plate Number 6.*

Another strange fact is that some Model 44-1894 rifles are found
with the 1885 barrel markings. I have not been able to find this 1885

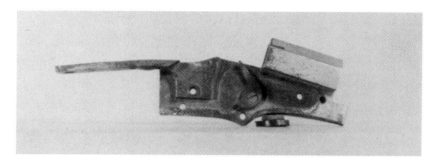

Plate Number 6   Portion of a "Sideplate" Stevens frame. (Photo: Edson Klinkel).

patent date pertaining to firearms, or improvements thereof, listed in the Patent Office Indices. Where do you go for references when the patent is not listed in the Index?

One of these '94 pattern rifles with the 1885 barrel markings is in the .22-20 caliber. This is the .22 Harwood cartridge illustrated in *Boys' Rifles.* The owner of this rifle also has an 1894 Stevens catalogue in which the .22 WCF cartridge is shown instead of the .22 Harwood which is shown in my 1894 catalogue. Apparently, there were at least two issues of this catalogue, as there are of so many other years, of Stevens issue.

The patent date may be like that of October 29, 1889, seen stamped on some Stevens barrels. It may not pertain to the firearm itself but to a manufacturing procedure. There is no record of this later patent date, either, so it may have been issued to someone else and purchased or used by Stevens, during this period of time. There were other patents issued to or used by Stevens, and I have obtained copies of these only to learn they pertain to certain machine tools. References to this pattern rifle are non-existent in the records of the old Walnut Hill Rifle Club, and all innovations introduced at this famous old range were well publicized, except the side plate models. It is almost as if everyone was sworn to secrecy until the 1894 model was introduced.

Plate Numbers 7 and 8 shows a small frame side plate rifle which differs somewhat from those reported before.

This small frame rifle is totally unmarked, but other than the action variance mentioned, is a smaller, but identical, mate to the 'large frame' rifles. Because of the machining necessary to the 'small frame' variances it would have to be more expensive to produce. I assume, therefore, it is reasonable to speculate that the small frame came first.

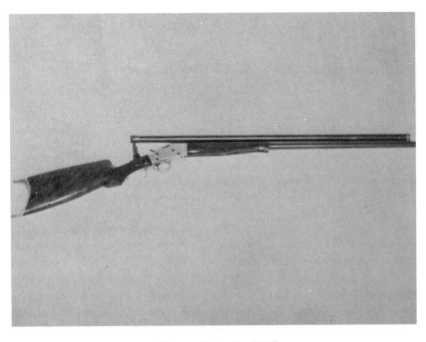

Plate Number 7   Stevens Small Frame "Sideplate" Rifle.

(Photo: David Cox Collection).

Explanation of *Plate Number 7:*
   Name of Rifle: Stevens
   Model: Deluxe 'small frame' side plate rifle.
   Serial Number: None
   Markings: None
   Caliber: .25-20 Single Shot
   Barrel Length: 24½" part round
   Sights: Has a 28" unmarked telescopic sight. Tang scope base
      has micrometer elevation and windage adjustments.
   Remarks: This rifle has a burl walnut stock with Stevens 'S'
      curve pistol grip. Has typical Stevens deluxe checkering on
      both grip and forend. The frame, lever and Swiss butt plate
      are nickel plated. The forward placement of the lever pivot
      screw requires an additional milling cut than has the more
      common side plate action. Presumably, this more
      expensive-to-produce side plate was earlier than, and
      abandoned in favor of, the more common side plate.

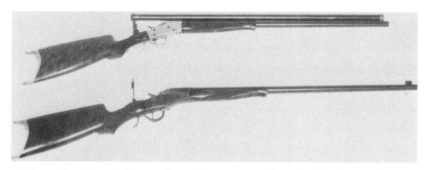

Plate Number 8 shows this rifle compared with the larger frame rifle. The larger frame deluxe version rifle, shown on *Plate Number 9* has the following specifications.

Name of rifle: Stevens

Model: Deluxe side plate model.

Serial Number: None

Markings: On side flat of the barrel: "J. Stevens A. & T. Co. Chicopee Falls, Mass., Pat'd. Aug. 11, 1885.

On the bottom flat of this barrel under the wood is stamped '16' which possibly is the twist used in the rifling.

Caliber: .25-20 Single Shot.

Sights: Stevens tang rear sight and fixed globe front. No rear barrel slot.

Remarks: Burl walnut stock with Stevens 'S' curve pistol grip. Grip and forend bear typical Stevens deluxe checkering. **Nickel-plated brass butt plate.**

Plate Number 9   Stevens Large Frame "Sideplate" Rifle.

(Photos: David Cox Collection).

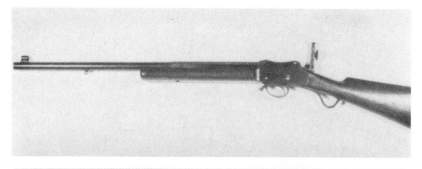

Plate Numbers 10 & 11   Stevens Bisley Model and markings.

(Photos: Michael Roberts).

Plate Number 10 shows a rifle I had heard rumors of before, but was unable to illustrate in previous books. This is a Martini system rifle, and the frame is stamped 'Stevens Bisley Model.' *Plate Number 11* pictures the marking on the side of the frame.

A letter dated December 6, 1961, from Roe S. Clark, Jr. of the Research & Development Department of Savage Arms Corporation, states that there is one of these Bisley Model rifles in the collection of the factory, but he could throw no light upon the model.

A later letter from Mr. Clark, under the date of January 12, 1962, has this to say:

"Just today I found a J. Stevens Arms & Tool Co. catalogue of 1910-1911 English edition and in it is the ad for the following:

'The Stevens-Bisley Model #600'

The "Modele Deluxe" miniature target rifle.

"This model specially made for the English market, has been brought out at the express wish of our many friends in the United Kingdom. It has the well-known Martini action, which is so easy to manipulate, especially when rapid firing. It is eligible for use in all competitions for Military Miniature Rifles."

Weight: With 27" bbl. 9 1/2 Lbs.

Barrel: Half octagon Stevens match quality.

12

Ammunition: Chambered and rifled for H.P.S. King's Norton .22 L.R. smokeless.

Action: Martini pattern, with under lever ejector, case hardened and special finish

Stock: Specially selected oiled walnut stock and forend, well figured, neatly checkered, with horn cap to forend. Engine-turned butt plate.

Sights: B.S.A. aperature rear sight with adjustable eye cup, and micrometer Wind Gauge and vertical adjustments. Combination ring and bead, Bead & Barleycorn, or Ring and Knife-edge fore-sight.

Extras:

Willesden or mail canvas covers	7/6 each
Patent slings	3/6 each

Price 5 Pounds 5 Shillings

While this describes the gun very accurately, it does not give us any information as to when it was introduced or for how long it was made. However, it is some knowledge and we have made a little progress. Perhaps later on I'll run across more information."

A letter from Parker-Hale Limited, Bisley Works, Birmingham, England, dated June 2, 1976, to the present owner of the rifle illustrated was unable to give any further information on this particular model.

The action of this Stevens Bisley Model is a typical British, large frame, Martini frame. Underside of the action in front of trigger guard is stamped "52." The front face of the frame is stamped 6 0 3 in tiny figures. Action frame and breech block have British proof marks.

The barrel is part octagon, 26" long. Bottom flat is marked 6X. The bottom of round portion of the barrel is marked "52" about 12½" from the muzzle. Right hand upper flat of barrel is marked with British Proof and 22L." The upper left hand flat is marked "J. Stevens Arms & Tool Company, Chicopee Falls, Mass., U.S.A."

There is also the remains of a number on bottom flat of barrel where the forearm lug is fitted. A tiny number "3" is still visible. It matches the "603" on the action. The buttstock is a typical British sporting Martini pattern of plain walnut. The bottom of the buttstock is stamped "ႬƐႬ" and how a number 734 can be stamped backwards baffles both the owner of this rifle, and me. The forend is semi-beavertail type and unmarked. The sights consist of B.S.A. tang rear mounted on the wood since there is no upper tang on the action. It also has an early Lyman 17 globe front sight with a non-interchangeable insert.

On page 45 of the February, 1969 issue of *GUNS MAGAZINE* is a short monograph by Kingsley Karnopp on this rifle. The rifle illustrated is practically identical to the specimen I show here, except there is a swivel eye present on the under side of the barrel a few inches ahead of the forearm tip. This appears to be the same type of dovetailed swivel eye for the hook-on Stevens carrying sling which was offered in some of the earlier Stevens catalogues. This is not a base for the usual military pattern shooting sling.

The article by Mr. Karnopp states: "The Rarest Stevens? Only ten of these rifles were made, according to O. M. "Jack" Knode, Vice President at Savage-Stevens-Fox. Thirty years ago when he first came to Stevens, the old timers told him that these ten were outlawed on the famous Bisley Range in England, because they were 'too accurate.' Jack says to take this with a grain of salt, but nonetheless that was the story the way he heard it.

"A typical, turn-of-the century, half-octagon, Stevens barrel in .22 rimfire caliber is mounted on a typical, heavy, British Martini action. The usual Stevens markings are on the barrel. The frame is engraved 'Stevens Bisley Model' ".

When I later saw King Karnopp at a meeting of the American Single Shot Rifle Ass'n., he told me he was not certain this rifle was authentic.

It's an interesting rifle, though not one of great beauty.

The early '94 Model 110 rifle mentioned above in .22-20 Harwood caliber, is serial numbered 2088 which seems to place it very near the side plate models, according to my survey. It would seem the numbers were consecutive from the side plates into (or through) the 1894 models. In relation to serial numbers it would appear that the Ladies Model Favorites were serial numbered separately from regular Favorite model issues, as one turned up with a three digit number and a central extractor.

The 1885 and 1889 patent dates seen on some rifles could be in the same category as that of the Nelson King and Sharps Rifle Company patent. Both claimed to have taken out a patent on the "half-cocking on opening the action" and there is no record of such a patent being issued. It seems questionable that a patent might exist, but not be listed in the Patent Office Index.

It's a pity none of the old Stevens factory records exist today. All records were destroyed shortly after World War One when Congress threatened to investigate the company's alleged illegal profiteering on World War One contracts.

On Page 418 of *Boys' Single Shot Rifles* there is a page from the 1894 Stevens catalogue, at least it was the 1894 catalogue I had at the time. Now I find there was at least one other '94 catalogue issued, differing somewhat from that particular one. This multiplicity of catalogues bearing the same date but differing in some respect is common with Stevens. Generally there were several issues of the same catalogue number in the later series issued by the company. Some are marked "Reprint Edition," others are not. So it is no wonder many collectors are thrown by this. It almost seems at times there was a conspiracy by this company to confound and mix up the later reader. Perhaps that is why we find this marque so fascinating?

Heading the list of early '94 pattern rifles is serial number 2262. This rifle has the sharply square corner at lower front joint of the frame with the barrel housing. It is a two barrel outfit, one is for the .25-25 Stevens cartridge, the other for the .32 Ideal cartridge. Both barrels are marked with the same number which appears on the lower tang of the receiver. There are no cuts on these barrels for a rear barrel sight, but there is a vernier tang rear sight on the action. No markings on the usual place at front end of receiver, however, the buttstock and forend wood are both marked with the number 262. The extractor is on its usual left hand side and the breech block has a tension screw installed. Bottom of barrels are marked: "107 32 2262." Top of barrel flat is stamped: "J. Stevens A & T Co., Chicopee Falls, Mass. U.S.A. Pat. Apr. 17, '94." The two matching barrels constitute a rather unusual Model 107.

Another early rifle, a model 109, is a two barrel outfit, also. It has barrels for the .22 Extra Long centerfire and for the .32 Ideal cartridge. These barrels have the usual '94 markings. The calibers and "109" are marked under the forend wood. Action frame has the early, square cut side walls with single pivot screws. The hammer of this action has the long adjusting screw from the top to the trigger for pull adjustment. Barrels have no slots for rear sight, but have open front sights and a Stevens tang vernier rear on the action.

Owned by the same Stevens collector, is another 44 with that Oct. 29, 1889, patent marking. This is a later 44 with rounding corners at frame junction with barrel housing portion. It has the usual half octagon barrel marked #2. The action, barrel and wood are all marked number 11523. It has the early side extractor. The 24-inch barrel is stamped "J. Stevens A. & T. Co., Chicopee Falls, Mass. Pat. Oct. 29, '89", and on the left barrel flat ".32 Long R.F." Note this one has no U.S.A. marking after the state mark. Just another attempt by Stevens to throw us off the trail, no doubt. This action has the lever and block pivoted on large screws entering from the left side. Some other actions have the smaller double screw system. This one merits the incredulous "huh?!" exclamation heard often, uttered when the collector spots Stevens variations.

This leads me into the rifles bearing the early model number designations. You know the pre-1900 catalogues listed several models which did not appear after 1903 when the 'new action' or 44½ type actions came into use.

Plate Number 12   (Photo: James R. Chunn)

Plate No. 12 shows a Model 46-44 series rifle, the description follows:

Model 46: Serial Number 3334.

Receiver: Nickel-plated, appears old and original.

Lever: No. 1 style and also plated.

Breech block: Color hardened. The hammer and trigger show old gold-plating. Single pivot screws. Serial number is on lower tang and is the older slant type letters. Extractor is early seven o'clock type. Receiver marked on front '46.'

Barrel: Blued, full octagon, 30". Serial number forward of forend and in the same slant style digits. Markings are on the top flat and are the normal 1894 style. Barrel is marked 1. Caliber stamped under the forend wood. Plain blade front and two leafed Lyman rear No. 6 as shown in Lyman catalogue of 1895. Tang sights same as shown as #33, Page 31 *Single Shot Rifles.* Stocks are plain grained walnut. Old Nickel-plate on the #2 Swiss butt plate. Palm rest is serial numbered on the base only, finish of wood matches that of the gun.

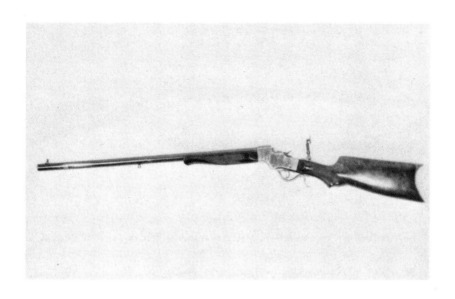

Plate Number 13   Stevens Model 47-44. (Photo: James R. Chunn).

Plate Number 13 illustrates a model Number 47-44 rifle. Receiver is color case-hardened, wide central extractor, not the kicking ejector. Double pivot screws for block and lever. Receiver has 47 stamped on front under the forend wood. Serial Number 17108 is stamped on lower tang. Barrel 26 inch full round. Markings on the barrel are on right hand side and upside down. Small lettering states "J. Stevens Arms Company, Chicopee Falls, Mass., U.S.A." There is a sling eye attachment on underside of the barrel ahead of the forearm tip. No rear slot for sight in barrel, combination folding front and Lyman folding rear tang sight. The stocks are of fancy walnut, finely checkered, and both are serial numbered. Butt plate is the rifle style also numbered. This rifle appears to be original throughout and is a very fine and intriguing piece.

Another Model 46 rifle is serial numbered 3896, which is in the ballpark serial number range of the Model 46 previously mentioned. This rifle has a #4 part octagon barrel, without a rear sight slot, 28 inches long and caliber is .38-55. Frame corners are the rounding pattern. Buttstock is the heavy style with No. 3 Swiss butt plate. It has a single trigger and the straight loop finger lever. This pattern lever is not common but was used with single triggers up into the 44½ series of models.

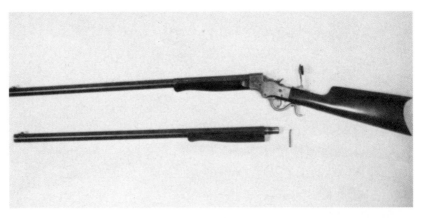

Plate Number 14   Stevens Model 109 with two barrels. (Photo: James R. Chunn).

Plate No. 14 illustrates a Model 109 rifle with two original barrels. One is .22 Long Rifle while the other is in caliber .32 Ideal, casehardened receiver with the sharp 90° cut sidewalls. Single pivot block and lever screws. Serial number on lower tang is 2629 in slant type digits. No model number or marks on front end of receiver. Barrels are 28″ part octagon with serial number ahead of forearms, again in slant type digits. The numbers 109 and calibers are marked on these barrels under the wood. The markings on top of barrel flats are the usual, normal 1894 pattern. No rear sight slots were cut into these barrels. Plain blade front sights and plain Stevens tang rear sight is like #31, Page 31, *Single Shot Rifles.* Stocks are of plain walnut, buttstock with iron rifle plate.

Still another Model 109 rifle is in Caliber .32-40. Model markings again on underside of the barrel, under the forend. Serial number is 2310. Frame has the typical square cut side walls. Side extractor is the early 1894 type. Barrel is 28″ part octagon, Number 2 in weight. Hammer is equipped with a trigger pull adjustment screw. The sights are No. 210 Globe front sight, spirit level in rear barrel slot and 104 Stevens tang rear sight. These sights are no doubt later replacements. The lever is the #5 Schuetzen type as usually found in the #51. The condition of this lever matches the rest of the rifle but could, of course, be also a later replacement. The buttstock appears to have a smaller than usual No. 3 Swiss nickel-plated butt plate. This plate is serial numbered same as the rest of the rifle, so appears to be original.

It may be possible these earlier 44 pattern action rifles start at about number 2000 and the regular no. 44's begin at about number 3000. But again we cannot make an intelligent guess about this due to the fact when one arbitrarily sets serial number ranges like this, he will soon be proven wrong by other specimens learned about later.

Plate Number 15   Stevens Model 50-44 with 23½ inch telescopic sight.

(Photo: James R. Chunn).

Plate No. 15 contains a fine model 50 in the 44 series. Receiver is color casehardened and etched with a rifleman on the left hand side, while right side shows a deer scene. Floral designs surround both scenes. Extractor is the early 7 o'clock side style and the frame has single pivot screws. Double set triggers and 4-finger loop lever. Serial number is 4666 on lower tang and the model number 50 appears on front of the receiver. Barrel is part octagon 30″, serial number forward of forend. Markings on top flat of barrel breech are the usual 1894 norm. Caliber marked under the forend wood and barrel also is marked #1. Rear sight on tang is like #32, page 31 *Single Shot Rifles.* No rear sight slot milled in barrel. Front sight is as #26, page 29 *Single Shot Rifles.* Barrel is milled flat for front offset mount for the telescopic sight which is numbered 595, 23½″ long. Stocks are of fancy walnut, finely checkered and serial numbered butt plate is the #3 Swiss type. Rifle appears to be entirely original with possible exception of the palm rest which may or may not be original to this rifle. This palm rest base appears to be that from a Winchester split-type or 'tuning fork' pattern rest used on some of the earlier Winchester Single shot Scheutzen rifles.

Plates Number 16 and 17 show other views of this fine target rifle.

Reports of Stevens 404 rifles built in the 44 type action continue to come in. Most follow the standard pattern with straight grip, small, shotgun buttstock, beavertail type forearm with checkering, while grip is uncheckered. One has a serial number of 61907. Another, numbered 61247, has a 28″ barrel for the .22 rimfire cartridge.

Plate Numbers 16 & 17 Close-up of Stevens Model 50-44. (Photos: James R. Chunn)

In the same serial number range is one numbered 61793 but this one has two barrels also with the same number, one for the .22 Long Rifle rimfire, 26"; the other 24" chambered for the .22 Short rimfire. Buttstock is of the usual shotgun-butt style and both barrels have the large checkered forearms. The sights consist of the usual Lyman side-of-receiver sight and one barrel has an open front while the .22 Short barrel has a hooded Lyman mounted on it. The front of the frame is marked; as two previously mentioned 404's i.e. '44 EX 00.'

A 404 built on the 44 1/2 type action differs somewhat from the general description of these rifles. This rifle has a 24" round barrel .810" at the muzzle, .950" at the breech. The barrel and lower tang are both numbered 11387. The lower tang bears the number 700 where these are usually stamped 404. I cannot account for this number instead of the regular model numbers and in much smaller and fainter stamped figures. Both barrel and receiver bear British proof marks, so possibly the 700 was placed upon the tang while in Britain. Another odd thing about this one is the fact the receiver is not drilled and tapped for the left side receiver Lyman sight. It has a

#210 globe front sight and a BSA tang sight mounted which bears the patent dates of 1907 and 1909. The original hard rubber shotgun butt plate is missing. This rifle sports the usual large checkered forearm and the sling or carrying swivel eye on underside of barrel ahead of the wood.

I have had called to my attention a specially-made Stevens on the 044 1/2 action. The story I hear is that this rifle was made for display at exhibitions and was never sold. The story also says the rifle was made in the 1890's, but I am sure this is an error since the 044 1/2 action was not produced till after 1900. The 044 1/2 action of this piece bears the number "50" on the front of the receiver, has engraving similar to the one shown on Page 42 of *More Single Shot Rifles* but is even more orante. Receiver, lever, breech block and butt plate are gold plated but frame has lost most of the gold. Very fancy grained walnut stocks, pistol grip buttstock and finely checkered. It has a single set trigger. There are two barrels and two matching forends. Both forends carry matching serial numbers of 2524. The .22 Long Rifle barrel has number 2524 to match and is #2 part round, part octagon. The .25-20 barrel has no serial number. Gun is complete in .22 rimfire caliber but the centerfire breech block and extractor for the .25-20 barrel are not with the outfit. The sights consist of a vernier tang rear with windage and a globe front sight on the .22 caliber barrel and Stevens Buckhorn rear with a combination Beach front sight. Quite a fine appearing little Stevens and very unusual!

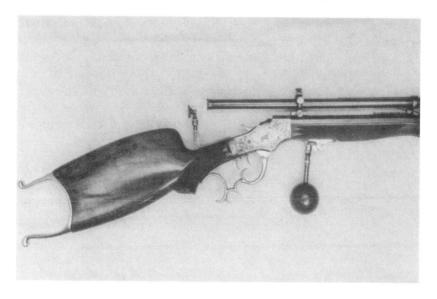

Plate Number 18   Stevens - engraved frame. (From Ralph Fields)

Plate Number 19 Stevens Model 0044 1/2 Special Order Rifle. (Photo: Brian Kent).

On Plate Number 18 is shown a beautiful Stevens in the Stevens Pope Special conformation with animal engraved frame.

Plate Number 19 illustrates a fine little rifle built on the 044 1/2 action, with double set triggers. The barrel, instead of the usual part octagon No. 1 weight, is of full octagon pattern. Stock is as apparent, a straight grip pattern with a rifle butt plate. The wood is well checkered in the usual careful manner accomplished by Stevens. The rifle mounts a Stevens telescopic sight in addition to a Beach combination front and Lyman tang rear sight. Not a model variation, but a rifle showing some of the options available from the old factory.

Stevens rifles with unusual markings continue to be found. How about a special order .45-44 1/2 Serial No. 11,268 in .32-40 (on the lower flat)? Upper flat has "STEVENS TRADE MARK, Pat. Appl. Off. & Fgn." No dates, city or state mentioned.

Here's a No. 52/44 1/2 Stevens-Pope, Serial No. 4654, 30" barrel in .22 short. Pope rifling, barrel number 15,1617 in the usual small numbers close to the action. Top barrel flat is stamped with the usual "J. STEVENS, A. & T. CO., Chicopee Falls, Mass." No Stevens-Pope stamping, yet is definitely such a rifle. The lower barrel flat is stamped "22 Short."

At a later date, I am now able to give the specifications of a very nice Stevens Model 110 rifle, which is shown on *Plate Number 20*. This Stevens No. 110 has the usual early type 44 action with the sharply cut shoulder and the side extractor. It is numbered 2368. The frame is color case hardened, but has the earlier mottled color pattern not the later ripple or marcel design of hardening. The hammer has the long screw extending down through to adjust the trigger pull. The owner reports that even when the pull is adjusted lightly it is fairly stable. Barrel is the half octagon, half round size in No. 2

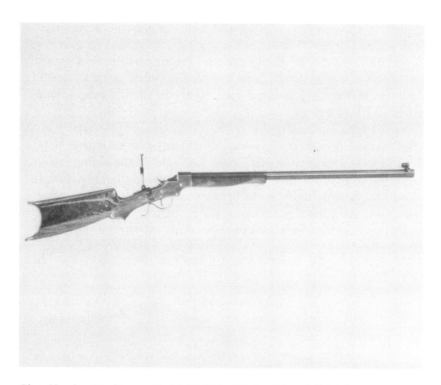

Plate Number 20   Stevens Model 110 Rifle. (Photo: Edward Haight)

and numbered 2368 just ahead of the forearm wood on the under side. Under the forearm wood appear 110 and 25-25. Has the usual Stevens marking of the period on top flat. The stock is made of very fancy walnut and has a pistol grip. The fancy checkering pattern is the two diamond size as seen on most of the pistol grip Tip-up models. The forearm, held with one screw, is also checkered to match. Butt plate is the No. 2 Swiss numbered 368. Front sight is a Beach combination, no rear barrel slot, and tang rear is a Stevens plain adjustment type sight. Weight of the rifle is 8 lbs., 5 oz. and it is, of course, a .25-25 caliber rifle. This is about the fanciest early model of this series we have been able to report.

I have photos and full descripton of a rather odd Stevens 44 1/2 rifle. The frame, while a 44 1/2, has no model numbers on it anywhere. It has the single trigger, loop, finger lever in a straight pattern. Since this rifle has a straight gripped stock, the lever would naturally be of this pattern. This straight loop lever is not met with too often, but I have seen several rifles so equipped, all with single triggers. Some of these single triggers have been of the single set variety, but to date I have not observed one of these straight levers with double set triggers.

Caliber of the barrel is .32-40 and it is 32″ long, part octagon, part round, serial number of the barrel and action is 11139. This barrel is stamped "Stevens-Pope" above the usual manufacturers stamping, and "Nickel Steel" on top right flat of the barrel, upside down. Rifling is Pope style, left hand gain twist. It has the long forend secured with two screws.

The buttstock and mid-point of the underside of this barrel have the Stevens swivel eyes for the hook-on carrying strap fittings.

To add to the interest of this piece, both sides of the action frame have in the center, an 'H' enclosed in an engraved diamond panel. This was apparently done at the Stevens factory as the frame shows much color hardening remaining, of the correct Stevens pattern. The initial 'H' is possibly one initial of the original owner and put there upon special order by this purchaser? See *Plate Number 20A.*

Plate Number 20A   (Photo: F. C. Magro).

Concluding the chapter on Stevens, here are a few tidbits that should be of interest. I have mentioned that the last listing of the Stevens Favorite was in 1937. However, another catalogue, the "75th Anniversary Catalog" with a price list dated 1939, shows the Model 27 at $9.75. The same catalogue also shows the pistol grip Model #26.

I have also mentioned seeing several Stevens Model #16 Crackshots with various trade names stamped on them. Now, we can add "The 22 Spencer, Pat. App'l. for" to this list. This name has been found on at least three rifles, all with that odd top tang mechanism. These rifles were NOT made by the company that manufactured the old Spencer repeating rifle of Civil War fame, contrary to some stories you may have heard.

II

Boys' Rifles

Page 586 of *Boys' Single Shot Rifles*, shows the little odd Clive rifle. Due to the fact this specimen came to me quite late I was unable to give much information on the piece at that time. Since *Boys' Rifles* was published in 1967 however, I have managed to obtain the copies of the original patent letters covering this system and show them on *Plates Number 21 and 22*.

Plates 23 and 24 show the text of the Patent claim. The patent paper drawings of the action show a great resemblance to the actual rifle shown on page 586 which does not always occur. The specimen illustrated previously shows an abbreviated hammer spur, this could have been shortened by an owner previous to me.

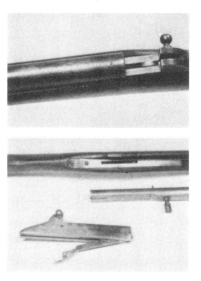

Plate Numbers 25 & 26   A. A. Clive Patent Rifle—Action opened and disassembled.

A. A. CLIVE.
BREECH LOADING FIREARM.

No. 592,196.

Patented Oct. 19, 1897.

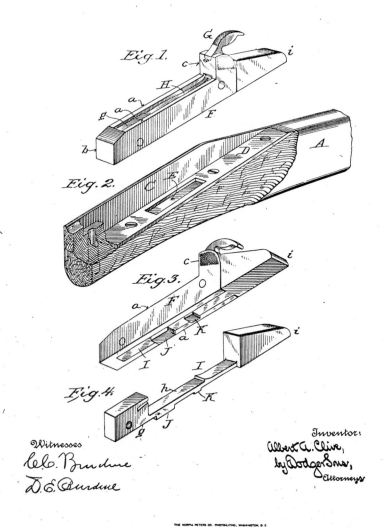

Fig. 1.

Fig. 2.

Fig. 3.

Fig. 4.

Witnesses

Geo. C. Bundine
D. E. Bundine

Inventor:
Albert A. Clive,
by Dodger Bros,
Attorneys

A. A. CLIVE.
BREECH LOADING FIREARM.

No. 592,196.

Patented Oct. 19, 1897.

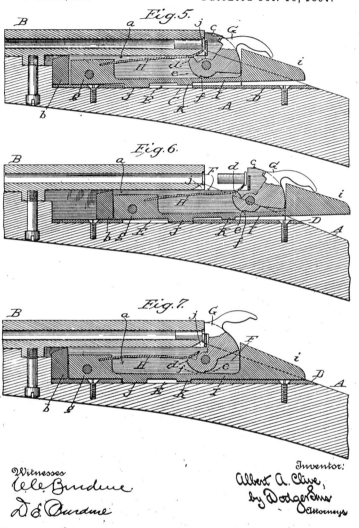

Fig. 5.

Fig. 6.

Fig. 7.

Witnesses

Inventor:
Albert A. Clive,
by Dodge Sons
Attorneys

United States Patent Office.

ALBERT A. CLIVE, OF ILION, NEW YORK.

BREECH-LOADING FIREARM.

SPECIFICATION forming part of Letters Patent No. 592,196, dated October 19, 1897.

Application filed June 28, 1897. Serial No. 642,682. (No model.)

To all whom it may concern:

Be it known that I, ALBERT A. CLIVE, a citizen of the United States, residing at Ilion, in the county of Herkimer and State of New York, have invented certain new and useful Improvements in Breech-Loading Firearms, of which the following is a specification.

My present invention pertains to improvements in breech-loading firearms, the construction and advantages of which will be hereinafter set forth, reference being had to the accompanying drawings, wherein—

Figure 1 is a perspective view of the breech-block, hammer, and attendant parts; Fig. 2, a similar view, partly in section, of so much of the gun-stock as is necessary to illustrate my invention; Fig. 3, a like view of the breech-block viewed from the under side; Fig. 4, a perspective view of the trigger, and Figs. 5, 6, and 7 sectional views illustrating the parts in their different operative positions.

The object of my invention is to produce a simple and compact gun, one which does away with any intricate lock mechanism and at the same time is efficient when in use.

In the drawings, A designates the stock of the gun, and B the barrel, secured thereto in a manner which will prevent it from moving thereon. In the upper face of the stock there is formed a recess or chamber C, open at its rear end, and in the bottom of which is secured a plate D, provided with an oblong slot or recess E. Mounted within the recess or chamber C is the combined breech mechanism, hammer, and trigger.

F denotes the breech-block as a whole, consisting of the side bars *a a*, connected at their forward end by a cross-bar *b* and at their rear end by the upwardly-projecting breech-block *c*.

G indicates the hammer, pivoted between the rear ends of the side bars *a*, its striking-point, when the hammer is down, occupying the position indicated in Figs. 1, 3, and 7. The hammer is of the form shown in Figs. 5, 6, and 7, provided with a nose *d* and a sear-shoulder *e*, the former acting in conjunction with spring H and the latter with a projection *f*, formed upon the trigger-plate I.

The trigger-plate (shown in detail in Fig. 4) comprises a block *g*, a plate *h*, and the trigger or thumb-piece *i*, all formed integral, as shown.

Block *g* is provided with a cross-slot in which is mounted the spring H, said spring extending rearwardly and bearing upon the nose of the hammer, its normal position being indicated in Fig. 7. It will be noted that the rear end of the spring is inclined slightly in an upward direction, and, when the gun is cocked, bears against the rim of the cartridge, as in Fig. 5. Inasmuch as the breech-block cannot be withdrawn unless the gun be cocked, as will presently appear, the spring acts as an extractor and forces the shell out of the barrel as the breech-block is drawn back. Upon reference to Figs. 5, 6, and 7 it will be noticed that the barrel is cut away at its rear end, forming a recess *j* to permit the spring to enter in front of the rim of the shell, as just stated.

The trigger-plate, which is pivoted between the bars *a*, as shown, is provided upon its under face with two lugs or projections J and K, the lug J being longer than the other and designed at all times to project into the slot E, its function being to limit the movement of the breech mechanism toward and from the rear end of the barrel, the extreme positions being indicated in Figs. 5, 7, and 6, respectively. The relation of the lug K to the slot E is such that said lug cannot enter the slot unless the breech-block is up against the rear of the barrel, in which position said lug comes into proper position to engage the rear wall of the slot, as shown in Figs. 5 and 7. When the parts are assembled, the breech mechanism is placed in the recess in the stock, the lug J entering the slot in the plate D. The barrel is then put in place, its under face bearing upon the cross-bar *b*, and a screw passed up through the stock into a lug formed on the barrel, as shown.

When it is desired to load the gun, the hammer is cocked, and by its movement the spring is elevated by the nose *d*, and the notch *e* engages the projection *f*, the trigger-plate at the same time being drawn up slightly, by reason of the elevation of the end of the spring by the nose *d*, into the position denoted in Fig. 1, in which position the lug K is withdrawn from the slot, permitting the breech mechanism to be drawn out into the position indicated in Fig. 6. So soon as there is the slightest rearward movement of the breech mechanism, the lug K bears upon the face of plate D, and consequently the trigger cannot be depressed to release the hammer, preventing the gun from being accidentally discharged. The act of withdrawing the breech-block withdraws the exploded cartridge from the barrel. A new shell is then inserted and the breech mechanism shoved forward to its closed position. It will be noted that it will be impossible to prematurely explode the shell, or until the breech-block is directly against the shell, for until the parts are in such position the lug K bears upon the plate D and the trigger cannot be depressed. When said lug comes over the end of the slot E, the trigger may be depressed, and when this takes place the lug K enters the slot, releasing the hammer and exploding the cartridge. Of course as the lug K enters the slot it engages the rear edge thereof, thus securely preventing the breech mechanism from being blown back by the explosion of the cartridge.

I claim—

1. In a gun, the combination of a stock; a recess formed therein opening toward the rear of the stock; breech mechanism mounted in and movable in and out of said recess; a hammer and a trigger carried by said breech-block; and a barrel secured to the stock extending back over the recess, holding the parts in place.

2. In a gun, the combination of a stock a recess formed therein opening toward its rear; breech mechanism mounted in and movable back and forth in said recess; a hammer, and a trigger carried by said breech mechanism; means for limiting the movement of the breech mechanism; and a barrel secured to the stock extending back over the recess, holding the parts in place.

3. In a gun the combination of a stock a recess formed therein opening toward its rear; breech mechanism mounted in and movable back and forth in said recess; a trigger and hammer carried thereby; means for limiting the movement of the breech mechanism; means for preventing the hammer from descending until the breech is closed; and a barrel secured to the stock extending back over the recess, holding the parts in place.

4. In a gun, the combination of a stock; breech mechanism mounted and movable back and forth thereon; a hammer; and a trigger and a spring for the hammer designed also to act as an extractor; the parts being carried by the breech mechanism.

5. In a gun, the combination of a stock; a recess formed therein; a slotted plate D secured to the bottom of the recess; and a breech mechanism mounted within said recess and provided with two depending lugs, one of said lugs remaining at all times within the slot and serving to limit the backward movement of the breech mechanism, and the second acting as a safety device to prevent discharge of the gun until the breech is closed.

6. In a gun, the combination of a stock; a recess formed therein; a slotted plate D secured to the bottom of the recess, a breech-block mounted in said recess; a trigger-plate pivoted in said block; and a lug depending from the trigger-plate and entering the slot in the plate.

7. In a gun, the combination of a stock; a recess formed therein; a slotted plate D secured to the bottom of the recess; a breech-block mounted in said recess; a trigger-plate pivoted in said block; and a short and a long lug depending from said plate and entering the slot, substantially as described.

8. In a gun, the combination of a stock; a recess formed therein; a slotted plate D secured to the bottom of the recess; a breech-block mounted in said recess; a trigger-plate pivoted in said block and provided with the depending lugs J and K; a hammer pivoted in the breech-block; and a spring carried by the trigger-plate, and bearing on the hammer.

9. In a gun, the combination of a stock; a recess formed therein; a slotted plate D secured to the bottom of the recess; a breech-block mounted in said recess; a trigger-plate pivoted in said block, provided with a long and a short depending lug designed to enter the slot in the plate; a hammer pivoted in the breech-block and provided with a notch e; a spring carried by the trigger-plate and bearing on the hammer; and a projection f formed upon the trigger-plate engaging the notch on the hammer when the same is cocked.

10. In a gun; the combination of a breech-block; a trigger-plate pivoted thereto; a hammer also pivoted to said block; and a spring carried by the trigger-plate and bearing on the hammer.

11. In a gun, the combination of a breech-block; a hammer pivoted at or near one end thereof; a trigger-plate pivoted at the opposite end acting in conjunction with the hammer, the trigger proper being located on the rear end of the trigger-plate in rear of the hammer; substantially as described.

12. In a gun the combination of a stock; a combined breech-block, hammer-and-trigger mechanism slidably mounted thereon; and a barrel secured to the stock over said mechanism, to retain it in place.

In witness whereof I hereunto set my hand in the presence of two witnesses.

ALBERT A. CLIVE.

Witnesses:
  Mrs. A. A. CLIVE,
  STEPHEN CLIVE.

Plates 25 and 26 show the top of action with block to the rear, preparatory to loading the cartridge and the action parts and barrel removed from the stock. This will give the reader who is unacquainted with this rifle an idea of the main component parts. This little rifle was evidently not too popular as they are very seldom seen today. I have seen only one specimen other than the one I owned before *Boys' Rifles* was published. However, in view of the unorthodox system employed it is not surprising the rifle did not succeed. Mr. Clive also patented a magazine gun in 1893, four years previous to this single shot mechanism in 1897.

Atlas Rifle Company, Ilion, New York.

Page 243 *Boys' Single Shot Rifles* contains some information on the little unlocked breech system Atlas rifle. At that time I was not sure any of these rifles were actually produced at Ilion, New York; however, since that time more rifles have come to my attention and I now am able to offer more information on them.

Plate Number 27 shows the paper drawing of the patent covering the Atlas gun, issued to G. P. Gunn.

Plates Numbers 28 and 29 illustrate the text of the patent papers granted to Mr. Gunn. Several rifles bearing the following barrel stamping have since come to light:

ATLAS GUN CO. ITHACA, N.Y., PAT'D. FEB. 18, 1890.

This is stamped on top of the barrel at breech end in letters about 1/16" high. Most of those observed have no caliber, etc. marked upon them. However, I have knowledge of at least one marked thusly: "DEAD SHOT 22 CALIBER RIFLE." Another specimen is stamped: "ATLAS RIFLE, PAT'D. MODEL 1906 FOR 22 SHORT BLACK POWDER CARTRIDGES ONLY." It is unknown at present time just when the Meriden, Connecticut, plant began manufacturing this rifle for Sears, Roebuck & Co.; but, obviously, it was sometime after the patent date of 1890. Witness the barrel stamping of the one listed above of "1906 Model." There are variations in these rifles, such as, some have 18" heavier round barrels. There are also variations in the extractor mechanism.

One examined had no spring in the extractor, and has a right angled lip going up the side of the chamber, i.e. OL. The number of Atlas rifles produced at Ilion or at Meriden is of course, unknown as no serial numbers have been observed on any specimen, so far. There is some conjecture that they were all produced at Ilion; however, this cannot be proven. Records of the old plant at Meriden have never been found, and most likely will not be found, at this date.

G. P. GUNN.
BREECH LOADING GUN.

No. 421,492. Patented Feb. 18, 1890.

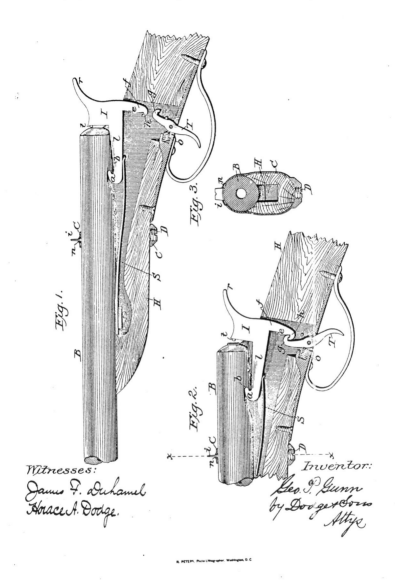

Witnesses:
James F. Duhamel
Horace A. Dodge.

Inventor:
Geo. P. Gunn
by Dodge & Sons
Attys

UNITED STATES PATENT OFFICE.

GEORGE PECK GUNN, OF ILION, NEW YORK.

BREECH-LOADING GUN.

SPECIFICATION forming part of Letters Patent No. 421,492, dated February 18, 1890.

Application filed September 10, 1889. Serial No. 323,536. (No model.)

To all whom it may concern:

Be it known that I, GEORGE PECK GUNN, a citizen of the United States, residing at Ilion, in the county of Herkimer and State of New
5 York, have invented certain new and useful Improvements in Breech-Loading Guns, of which the following is a specification.

My invention relates to breech - loading guns; and the invention consists in certain
10 novel features of construction, as hereinafter set forth.

Figure 1 is a side elevation with the stock shown in section. Fig. 2 is a similar view showing the hammer in a different position,
15 and Fig. 3 is a transverse vertical section on the line x x of Fig. 1.

This invention relates to that class of guns which use small metallic cartridges and which are used for target practice and the like,
20 and the object is to cheapen the construction and to render the gun more safe in handling and prevent accidents.

In the accompanying drawings, B represents the barrel, secured to the stock H by a
25 band C and by a shoulder at the front end of the spring S, as shown in Fig. 1. In the under side of the barrel a short distance from its rear end I cut a notch, as shown in Figs. 1 and 2, in such a manner as to form a hook-
30 shaped shoulder b on the rear wall of said notch for the engagement of the front end of the combined breech-block and hammer I. This combined breech-block and hammer I make somewhat in the form of a letter T, the
35 central portion l being made of the proper length to reach from the rear end of the barrel to the notch, and having a hook a formed on its front end to engage with the shoulder b, as shown clearly in Figs. 1 and 2. It is
40 provided with a thumb-piece r and below that with an enlargement, the front face of which constitutes the breech-block, it being of the proper size to cover the bore and the head of the cartridge when closed or in the
45 position shown in Fig. 1. At its rear end it is provided with a downwardly-projecting arm f, as shown in Figs. 1 and 2, the lower end of which terminates in a hook h, which is arranged to engage with a similar hook g
50 on the upper end of the trigger T, as shown in Fig. 2, the interlocking of these hooks rendering it impossible to fire the gun while the

parts are in this position, either by pulling the trigger or by accidentally hitting the same.
55 It is also provided with a firing-point t, as shown in Figs. 1 and 2.

A short distance above the hook h on the front face of the arm f, I form a shoulder e, the face of which stands at or nearly at a
60 right angle to the arm f, on which the point of the hook g of the trigger T engages when the hammer is depressed to full-cock, and from which it is readily disengaged by a pull on the trigger when it is desired to fire the
65 gun.

To hold the combined hammer and breech-block in position and operate the same, I secure to the under side of the barrel a nearly straight, flat, and stiff spring, the front end
70 of said spring being fastened to the barrel by a clamp and screw, as shown in Fig. 1, the front ends of the spring and clamp forming a shoulder which abuts against a corresponding shoulder formed by cutting a recess in
75 the stock at that point, as shown in Fig. 1, and which prevents any forward movement of the barrel upon the stock, while the band C clamps the barrel firmly to the stock, as hereinafter more fully described. The rear
80 end of the spring S is made to bear upon the under side of the arm l of the combined breech-block and hammer I at a point some distance in rear of the shoulder b, and is curved or may have its point thickened and rounded, so
85 as to move freely on the arm l when the latter is depressed or raised.

The trigger T is pivoted in the usual manner, and is provided with a spring o to throw it back to the proper position to engage with the
90 hook h and the shoulder or sear-notch e, the rearward movement of the upper end of the trigger T being so limited, either by the shoulder or front wall of the slot in the guard-strap, to which it is pivoted, or by a pin in rear of
95 it above its pivot as to hold its upper end in the proper position to automatically engage with the hook h or the shoulder e when the hammer is depressed.

The band C is constructed in such a man-
100 ner as to hold and permit of the lateral adjustment of the sight i, and also clamp the barrel to the stock. To do this I make the band with a slot n at the top where it rests upon the top of the barrel, as shown in

Figs. 1, 2, and 3, there being a slight recess formed on the inside of the band along each side of the slot, as shown in Figs. 1 and 2. The sight *i* is made to project through the slot in the band, and is provided with small lateral flanges at its lower edge, (and which are readily formed by slightly upsetting the metal by means of suitable dies,) these flanges fitting in the recesses at the sides of the slot, as shown in Figs. 1 and 2, but so that the band will bear upon them and when drawn down tight hold the sight securely in position. As indicated in Fig. 3, the slot *n* is made longer than the width of the sight, so as to permit the sight to be adjusted to one or the other side when the band is loosened. At its lower side the band C is made much thicker, as shown in Figs. 1 and 2, it being provided at this point with a screw-hole to receive a large flat-ended screw D, the inner flat end of which bears against the under side of the stock, and thus draws the band down tight upon the barrel, thereby clamping the sight tight upon the barrel and the barrel firmly to the stock. When it is desired to adjust the sight, the screw is turned back a little, when the sight is free to be moved to the right or left in the slot *n*, after which, by tightening up the screw again, the parts are clamped in position.

I am aware that a combined hammer and breech-block has before been used; but in such cases it has been customary to pivot it to a lug projecting downward from the barrel. Such a construction adds to the cost of manufacture, and, besides, is not as safe, because the pivot-point is necessarily thrown much farther below the line or axis of the bore, thereby increasing the tendency of the breech-block to be thrown open by the explosion of the charge. By my construction it will be seen that the point of contact between the point of the hook *a* and the shoulder *b* is brought very nearly in line with the axis of the bore, and that, therefore, there is much less tendency of the breech to fly open when the gun is fired. The interlocking of the trigger-hook *g* with the hook *h* of the hammer also adds materially to the safety of the arm, and the simplicity of the construction enables the gun to be made very cheaply.

Having thus described my invention, what I claim is—

1. In combination with the barrel B, having the shoulder *b*, formed by a notch or recess in its under side, the combined hammer and breech-block I, provided with the hook *a* to engage with said shoulder, and the spring S, all arranged to operate substantially as shown and described.

2. The combination, in a gun, of the combined hammer and breech-block provided with the hook *h*, and the trigger T, provided with the hook *g*, said parts being arranged in relation to each other substantially as shown and described.

3. In combination with a gun-barrel and its stock, the band C, provided with the screw D, having its end arranged to bear against the stock, substantially as and for the purpose set forth.

4. In combination with the band C, provided with a slot, the sight *i*, constructed to fit and be adjustably held in said slot, with a screw D for tightening the same, substantially as set forth.

5. The combination, in a gun, of a barrel and an underhung combined hammer and breech-block united to the barrel by means of the hook *a* and shoulder *b*, as set forth.

In witness whereof I hereunto set my hand in the presence of two witnesses.

GEORGE PECK GUNN.

Witnesses:
A. D. RICHARDSON,
CHAS. HATTER.

While on the subject of the Meriden plant, I'd like to show a photo of an actual Meriden Model 6 rifle, since in *Boys' Rifles* a catalogue illustration was used. *Plate Numbers 30 and 31* show this specimen. This piece displays the usual 'flat board' stock and forend. It has a round barrel 22 3/16" long, .22 rimfire caliber. Dovetailed, flat steel, notched rear sight and a bead front sight. This rifle has the same action used on the Model 10 Meriden rifle. The top tang is drilled for a tang sight with holes spaced 1 1/8" center to center. Rifle has no markings other than "Meriden Firearms Co., Model 6". It is 37" long overall, and no butt plate ever graced the stock of this specimen. You may note I did not say *all* Model 6's lacked a butt plate? Some number 6's have color case hardened frames. Some were blued.

Plate Number 30   The Meriden Model 6 Rifle.

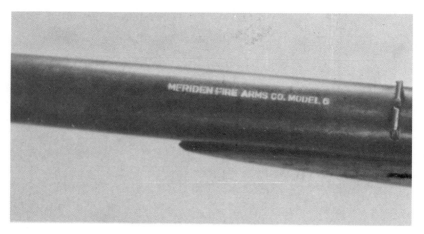

Plate Number 31   The Meriden Model 6 barrel marking.

34

Plate Numbers 32, 33 and 34 illustrate an interesting little rifle called Empire State Cadet Rifle. The specs of this concealed hammer Belgian rifle are given here:

Name of Rifle: Empire State Cadet

Maker: Unknown

Serial Number: 208 on barrel near breech.

Marked: Left side of frame: Empire State Cadet in script letters. On left side of barrel at breech appears the Belgian proof mark, ELG in an oval. Near this is a small star stamping and the letter "F."

Action type: An odd rolling block pattern, operated by a locked-up finger lever, concealed hammer. Lever lock is released by squeezing together spring lock lever and tail of finger lever. Trigger is pinned to the rear inside wall of frame and engages and thus cocks the concealed hammer when lever is closed. Extractor is pinned to inside front wall of frame and rotates on the lever axle screw.

Caliber: .32 Extra Short Rimfire. This uses the same tiny cartridge as the palm pistols.

Barrel length: 25¼ inches. Full round.

Length overall: 39½ inches.

Butt Plate: Small, smooth, iron shotgun type with short pointed top lip.

Sights: Small blade front, no rear sight is present nor is there any provision for one.

Frame: Original finish is indistinguishable today.

Factory original: Yes.

Takedown: No.

Remarks: The barrel is secured to the frame by a screw threaded up into lower side of the barrel through an extension projecting forward from the frame and integral with the frame. A pin through the frame from side to side also secures the breech of the barrel as well as anchoring the extractor.

Plate Number 32 Empire State Cadet Rifle (Photo: Edson Klinkel).

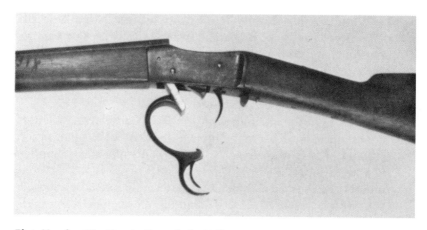

Plate Number 33   Empire State Cadet Rifle—action open.
                        (Photo: Edson Klinkel Collection).

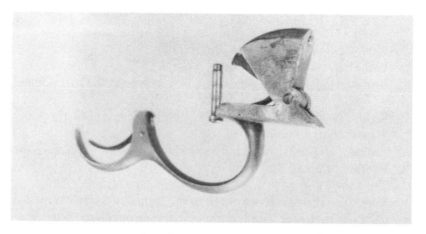

Plate Number 34   Empire State Cadet—Lever and block removed.

This rifle has a well designed stock typical of Belgian boys' rifles of the period. The wood used is European walnut. The forearm is secured to the barrel by means of three narrow iron barrel bands. Sling swivels of a curious round ring pattern are present. (Note full length view of rifle.) All in all, an interesting little rifle built on an unusual hammerless action design. The hammerless feature itself, since the rifle lacks a safety of any kind, may have prevented the wide spread popularity of the Empire State Cadet. This is the only example of this particular model I have examined but the owner of this one has seen one other specimen.

Plate Number 35 illustrates the breech mechanism dismounted from the frame of this rifle.

Plate Number 35   Breech Mechanism—Empire State Cadet Rifle.

Assorted Belgian Floberts

Plate Number 36 illustrates a Belgian Flobert rifle with double set triggers. These rifles so equipped were shown in some of the old wholesale catalogues but this is the only specimen I know of at this time. This rifle weighs 10½ lbs. and has a barrel 29 5/8″ long. It has an overall length of 47½″ from muzzle to toe of butt plate. The barrel is engraved: "J. VISER-HOFLEVERANCIER-DEVENTER." Stamped near the breech is the word "REGLE." The barrel has Belgian proof marks. The front sight has windage adjustment while rear sight is a replacement. There is a palm rest built into the trigger guard. This rifle can only be fired with CB caps, as a .22 Short will blow the breech open. Now you can truthfully state there were some made with double set triggers, for here is the proof! Close-ups of the dismounted trigger plate are on *Plate Number 37,* while the opened breech of the rifle is on *Plate Number 38.* Profile of the extractor looks like Mickey Mouse but it works well.

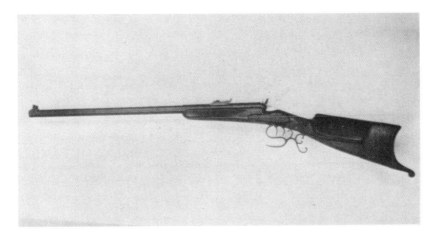

Plate Number 36   Set trigger Flobert Rifle. (Photo: John R. Allington).

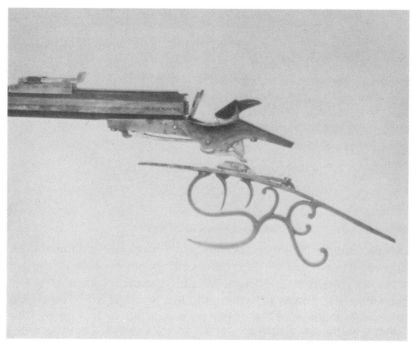

Plate Number 37   Close-up of breech section with double set trigger assembly dismounted.

Plate Number 38   Open breech section of Flobert Rifle showing unusual "Mickey Mouse" configuration of extractor.

38

Another interesting Flobert pattern rifle is illustrated on *Plate Number 39*. This shows the opened breech block of a concealed hammer Flobert rifle. It is built on the sloping block actions we usually refer to as the 'Springfield Flobert System' mainly because it operates by lifting and throwing forward like the 'trapdoor' Springfield action. Only in this case there is no hammer visible at the rear of the breech block. This piece has a 24″ full octagon barrel 15/16″ at breech, 7/8″ at muzzle. This barrel is marked: 'SELF EJECTING HAMMERLESS' on top flat near the breech. This lettering is in slanted gold inlaid letters. At least, I assume it is gold as it is still in bright gold color and brass would have long ago tarnished to be indistinguishable from the barrel iron. On the bottom flat of the barrel, under the wood are the letters "JG" and farther forward is "1407." On the left side of the barrel at rear is an eliptical panel containing the following: "G.D.—521—Patent". At the breech are the usual Belgian proofs of ELG in an oval; also a small star with the figure 7 below it. This rifle has the usual Flobert, well-designed buttstock with a round-end pistol grip. Checkered at grip and forward portions for a forend grip. An examination of the photo will show the concealed hammer projecting from the standing breech. After the rifle is fired, the block throws forward, and ejects the fired .22 shell.

Flobert Belgian-made rifles will be found with some other strange names upon them. One, a Pieper style, has the name "Hartford Arms Co's. Rifle" on the barrel; and, on the side ahead of the breech is the word "BISCOHA." Also Belgian proof marks such as the usual ELG in an oval with a star below the letters. Stamped on this barrel too, is a crown with the letter "U" below it. The rifle has a rather heavy full octagon 24″ barrel with a bore larger than .32 caliber. The stock is straight grip pattern with checkering at grip and forward end.

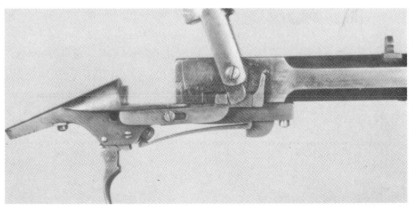

Plate Number 39   Open breech section of a "Hammerless" Flobert Rifle. Built on a sloping block action usually referred to as "Springfield Flobert System."

Remington Notes

Switching the subject to Remington Boys' rifles, perhaps you have noticed that some of the Remington Model 6 Improved have a black or blue lacquer applied to the frame or barrel (some are lacquered on both parts). Serial number 493812 rifle is so treated. Another, serial number 462585, had black or blue paint on the barrel, frame and trigger guard. It seems odd that a maker of guns the quality grade of Remington Arms would stoop to *painting* guns instead of the customary bluing.

One other which has turned up has a black lacquered barrel and *blued* frame. Some pieces are pretty well mixed up in finish, having color case-hardened blocks and trigger, blued receiver and butt plate, and a lacquered barrel.

Townleys Little Pal

In a 1935 wholesale catalog from Townley Metal & Hardware Company, Kansas City, Missouri, there is listed a "Little Pal" rifle. It is shown and described just above the cut and description of the Iver Johnson 2-X Safety Rifle. This is apparently identical to the 2-X Safety Rifle, with the exception of checkering; and, it had a chrome-plated bolt, according to the catalogue description.

In this same catalogue are listed Western Arms Company guns. The only gun pictured is a double barreled shotgun with the name plainly visible on the barrel "Western Arms Corp., Ithaca, New York," *including* the quotation marks.

Japanese Boys' Rifles

Here are two rifles from far off Japan. The first one, the Japanese copy of the Model 27 Hamilton was mentioned in *Boys' Single Shot Rifles*. The rifle is pictured here on *Plate Number 40A*. On *Plate Number 40*, I picture a piece of literature from the importer of the rifle, Nevada Sporting Goods.

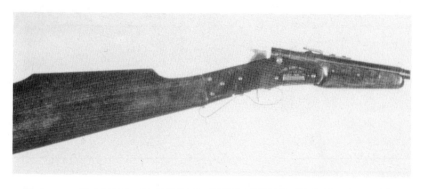

Plate Number 40A   Japanese copy of the Hamilton Model 27 Rifle.

Plate Number 40

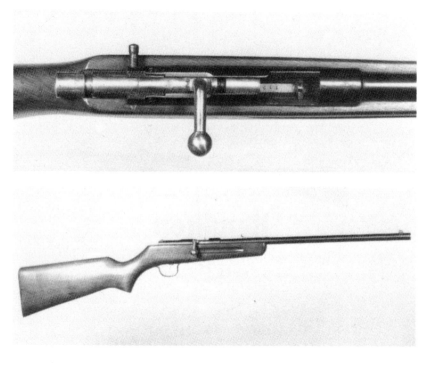

Plate Number 41   (Photos: Edson Klinkel).

Plate Number 41 illustrates another Japanese made rifle. A small and rather well fabricated bolt action .22 rifle. This has a 17 5/8″ round barrel rifled with 4 equal grooves and lands. It has a sliding extractor under the barrel similar to that employed on the Winchester model 1902 rifle. There is an unusual and positive safety at rear of the bolt which, when turned to the right, cams back the bolt head. Thus the trigger may be pulled freely without firing the rifle. The bolt cocks upon the closing stroke. Serial number at left side of breech and on the extractor is 1126. There are blade front and simple elevating rear barrel sights. Barrel is marked on left side: "MODEL AR-10 Cal. 22 Rifle, Made in Japan." The top of the receiver ring is stamped with a design consisting of three crossed arrows and the word "SAR" below. Marked on right side of the barrel is "SHINRISWAAIR   RIFLE MFG. CO.", (spaced as shown).

Another foreign-made single shot boys' rifle was made in Germany and imported by a Chicago, Illinois company. This is a copy of the Hoban bolt action which was illustrated and discussed in *Boys' Rifles*. These specimens are usually marked "United Arms Company, Chicago" and "United Seal of Quality." A rather showy military styled .22 rimfire rifle and reported to be a good shooter. They are scarce too.

42

Ross Rifle Company

Plate Number 42 shows another foreign made gun. This is the Ross Rifle Company single shot rifle built on a modification of the famous Ross straight pull action. This rifle has a 21½" round barrel. The top of the receiver is marked "Ross Rifle Company, Canada 1912." The side of receiver is stamped "Patented." There are various proof marks on rear of the barrel and on the receiver. Serial number 11799 is on the side of the barrel at breech. The tops of the two 'ones' did not stamp clearly so it is difficult to tell if they are really part of this serial number at all. Front sight is a flat topped post in a dovetailed, hooded type. The rear sight is an ingenious peep sight on the rear of receiver. Releasing a catch on right side of receiver extension allows a portion holding the sight to revolve, exposing the elevation adjustment screw on underside of this revolving part. Screwing off the sight-holding piece at rear of receiver allows the bolt to be withdrawn when the trigger is held back. It's a good sighting system.

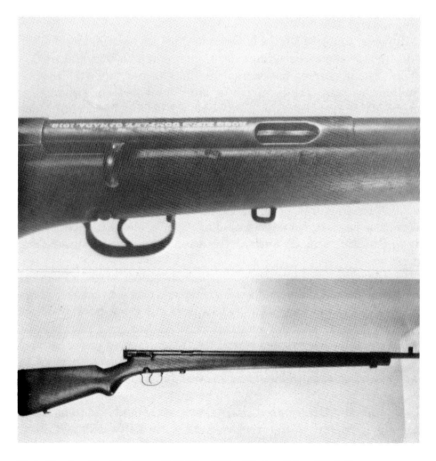

Plate Number 42   The Ross .22 Caliber Rifle. (Photos: Edson Klinkel).

The release in front of the trigger guard allows the bolt to be opened after the piece is loaded without pulling the trigger. This rifle has a military styled stock with front end extending to within 3" of the muzzle. Overall length of the rifle is 39½". A stacking swivel is in the fore tip band. A swivel is 3½" ahead of trigger and another, 2½" from toe of the stock. Trap butt opening is an iron military style butt plate for cleaning rod . . . no rod is present. The bolt release is in front of the trigger guard. Cross bolt safety is just above the trigger.

Page-Lewis

Just a few notes now on the Page-Lewis series of rifles discussed in *Boys' Single Shot Rifles*.

Some of the rifles in this A-B-C series of lever action single shot rifles have levers forged in one piece and not welded from two pieces. An Olympic Model C rifle I once owned had the welded-up lever and was serial numbered 2459. It was marked, as Page 278 *Boys' Rifles* states, "Pat. Appl'd. for."

However, another Model C Olympic rifle has the serial number of 2461 and has a one-piece finger lever and is marked "Pat'd. April 25, 1923." The suggestion has been made that the later rifle with a serial number just two digits higher is the "perfected" or production model. The finger levers of the few observed in one piece form are rounded in cross section more than the welded-up variety and a little more comfortable to the hand. Otherwise, I detect no other particular manufacturing differences. All Page-Lewis lever actions I have seen have the frame assembled from three or more pieces of steel riveted together and not forged-milled; however, I am careful to say here and now, some may have been made of a one-piece forging or casting. None of these Page-Lewis lever action rifles are very plentiful, and of course, the actual production figures are unknown.

A little more plentiful may be the bolt action Model D which originated in the old Page-Lewis Company and was continued in practically the same form after Savage acquired the company. When made by Page-Lewis, this bolt action model was generally marked Model D. Some are marked Model 50. When revived under Savage ownership the same few seem to have been marked D (carry over parts?), and then they were later marked Model 50 and also, Model 48.

I saw a bolt action marked "Page Lewis, etc.," and ".22 Long Rifle Model 50." At rear of the receiver is stamped 'KING NITRO.' Bolt was missing from the specimen. I have seen two or three of these

Page-Lewis rifles with the bolt missing. Why? Did they wear out and were discarded, or were they lost?

Another small bolt action single shot rifle whose action is identical to the Page-Lewis Model D, has a flat board stock and no butt plate ever. This rifle bears the name of "SPRINGFIELD ARMS CO., CHICOPEE FALLS, MASS." It has "Reliance" stamped on the frame opposite the bolt handle and it is also marked "Model D."

In the 1932 Stevens catalogue the rifle and parts are listed as "22 Long Rifle Model D Reliance Single Shot." It is obvious the Springfield Arms Co. was our old friend, Stevens, hiding beneath an alias.

Here's one more specimen to add to our list of rifles marked with distributor proprietary names. This rifle shown on *Plate Number 43* is obviously a Hopkins & Allen model. This frame is marked on the left side "Bull Frog Sr." with a likeness of a frog between the words "bull" and "frog." The frame is stamped on the front 922.

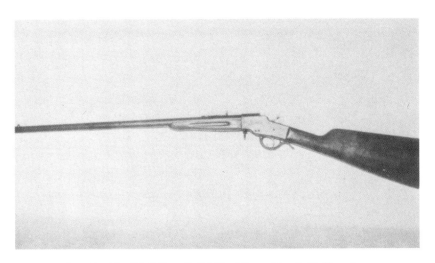

Plate Number 43   The "Bull Frog Sr." Rifle. (Photo: Ray E. Hoffman).

Rau Arms Corporation

Ever see a Wildcat .22 rifle? If not, look at *Plate Number 44* and see the "Wildcat Deluxe Model 600." The hang tag from this rifle is shown on *Plate Number 45* and, as it states, these rifles were made by the Rau Arms Corp. of Eldorado, Kansas. The opposite side of the frame is stamped "Rau Arms. Corp., Eldorado Kans., U.S.A." These rifles were built in the early 1970's.

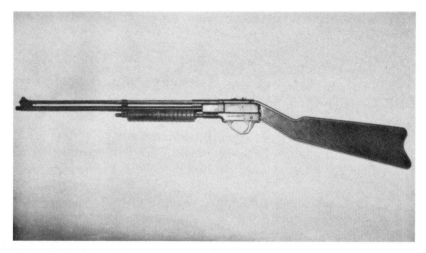

Plate Number 44   The Rau "Wildcat" .22 Deluxe Model 600.

(Photo: Ray E. Hoffman).

Plate Number 45   Hang tag from the Rau "Wildcat" .22 Deluxe Model 600.

(Photo: Ray E. Hoffman).

III

Hopkins and Allen

When *Boys' Single Shot Rifles* was in preparation, I couldn't locate any literature pertaining to the H & A noiseless rifle. All the H & A catalogues available omitted any reference to the model. Since then, however, some notices of the rifle have appeared.

Due to the kindness of Bob Kittrell of the South Carolina Arms Collectors Association we are able to present *Plate Number 46*, a photo copy of the original advertising sheet which was inserted loose into a H & A catalogue bearing the copyright date of 1914. On the back of this sheet was the Scout Military Model. This is shown on *Plate Number 47.*

At about this time, various Military or Cadet rifles were offered by several makers of boys' rifles. I refer to the Remington Boy Scout or Military model, Hamilton Cadet, etc., etc. The reproduction dated 1915 is from a catalogue of Iver Johnson Sporting Goods Company which is shown on *Plate Number 48.*

It is not known at present how long a life production the noiseless model enjoyed, but it may have had an early demise since its advent was after 1910. It may have been a victim of World War One since many civilian firearms models were discontinued when most factories were converted, or were converting, over to war munitions to supply that conflict. At any rate, specimens of this model are quite scarce. I did give the serial number of a rifle in *Boys' Rifles* and since then have seen another which has the number 222. It is very likely these noiseless rifles were serial numbered in a special series of their own.

Here's a New One

Hopkins & Allen Noiseless Rifle

THE latest success in a Noiseless shooting rifle, 22 calibre, 26-inch barrel. Shoots 22 short, long and long rifle **smokeless** cartridges.

NO NOISE!

NO SMOKE!

NO FLASH!

NO RECOIL!

Shoots and silences perfectly the explosion. Just the thing for indoor rifle practice, in that it can be used in the house without startling the occupants.

For outdoor use for small game it cannot be surpassed, for if you shoot and miss, the game is not frightened away, but there to shoot at again.

Especially desirable for ladies and beginners, as it entirely eliminates the natural tendency to flinch at the report.

A very neat and efficient little rifle with noiseless attachment which is a part of the barrel. No coupling to mar its neatness or symmetry. Does not differ in appearance from a regular rifle barrel, but it does the work, and like all Hopkins & Allen guns, it **shoots straight.**

Buy it from your dealer. Price, $7.50

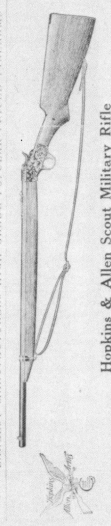

Hopkins & Allen Scout Military Rifle

THE necessity and importance of every young man and boy being acquainted with the handling and shooting of Military Arms is becoming more and more apparent every day.

The value of the "Boy Scout" movement is being universally recognized in the leading countries of the world. The demand for a military type rifle, shooting 22 calibre cartridges that is accurate, effective and at the same time cheap, is acknowledged almost everywhere.

To satisfy this requirement, we illustrate herewith a single shot Military type 22 calibre rifle. This rifle shoots accurately, and in every way accomplishes the purpose sought.

For practice, even in the militia, a 22 calibre saves greatly on ammunition as compared with the cartridges for large calibre guns, and will in the course of a year almost amount to the cost of the rifle itself. Every boy and young man should have this rifle. It is the **IDEAL** gun for making good soldiers.

DETAILED DESCRIPTION

The Hopkins & Allen Scout Military Rifle is equipped with the **Safety Stop Action.** The Hammer rests at **Safety Notch** and cartridge cannot be prematurely discharged. Solid Breech Block Action, Coil Springs. Round Blued Steel Barrel, 26 inches long. Case Hardened Frame and Mountings. Oil'd Machine Turned Military Half Pistol Grip Stock, fitted with Musket Forearm. Blued Steel Butt Plate. Leather Sling Strap. Open Front and Rocky Mountain Adjustable Rear Sights. Single Shot.

No better gun than this Military Rifle can be made for making good soldiers out of young men and boys, and at our low price it is one of the best bargains ever offered by an American Firearms Manufacturer. It will give delight to any boy or young man who is fortunate enough to possess it, and even men of mature years will find great pleasure in handling it. It shoots right where you aim every time, and is just as good for ordinary game and target shooting, as it is for the use of the soldier. This rifle shoots 22 short, long and long rifle cartridges. Weight each 4½ lbs.

40A

HOPKINS & ALLEN NOISELESS RIFLE

The latest success in a **noiseless** shooting rifle, 22 calibre, 26 inch barrel. Shoots 22 short, long and long rifle **smokeless** cartridges.

Shoots and silences perfectly the explosion.

Just the thing for indoor rifle practice, in that it can be used in the house without startling the occupants.

For outdoor use for small game it cannot be surpassed, for if you shoot and miss, the game is not frightened away, but there to shoot at again.

Especially desirable for ladies and beginners, as it entirely eliminates the natural tendency to flinch at the report.

A very neat and efficient little rifle with noiseless attachment which is a part of the barrel. No coupling to mar its neatness or symmetry. Does not differ in appearance from a regular rifle barrel, but it does the work, and like all Hopkins & Allen guns, it **shoots straight.**

Price $7.50

When you examine the silencer part from the front end, the inserts show a hole in the center for passage of the bullet, and spaced at regular intervals around this are eight small holes about 1/16″ in diameter. The front end of the silencer is roll crimped so it is not possible to dismantle the apparatus to examine the inside parts.

A friend of mine, Don Leech, did thoroughly examine one, however, and informed me the inside parts consist of 19 cups or cones. They are all shaped the same way, i.e. in cup form and all have the eight smaller holes around the central larger one. The interior of this silencer tube is 21/32″ in diameter, outside of the tube being 3/4″ in diameter. As mentioned before, the tube is 6 3/4″ long overall and the rear 1 3/16″ of the tube is threaded to screw onto the barrel. Don mentioned he dismantled the silencer years ago therefore was able to supply a drawing of it. He also remembered the silencer was not very effective.

Plate Number 49 is another page from the 1915 Iver Johnson Sporting Goods Catalogue showing among other items, a Maxim Silencer. This looks like the same silencer of which I owned two specimens years ago.

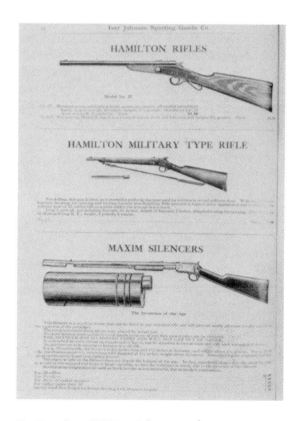

Plate Number 49   Page from 1915 Iver Johnson catalog.

I once owned a Maynard Model 15 rifle which had several original barrels with it. They were of various calibers and the .22 rimfire barrel had a silencer of the Maxim appearance on it. The muzzle of the barrel had a fitting permanently attached (threaded?) to it onto which the silencer proper threaded. This rifle was traded off to obtain a multi-barreled outfit in much better shape.

Later, I obtained a Bullard single shot rifle in .22 caliber also fitted with such an attachment. We shot both these rifles but found as most people do, that the .22 rimfire cartridges do not push their bullets fast enough to be much affected by these silencers. I never acquired another rifle with such an attachment till my H & A Noiseless specimen came along in mid-1961. After photographing it for *Boys' Rifles* it, too, passed on to other hands.

One of the H & A progenitors turned up recently. This is a Bay State Arms Company .32 rim-or centerfire caliber piece with a serial number of 559. It appears to be very similar to Plate 152 with a rear sight like that shown on Page 162. Both plates are in *Boys' Rifles*, of course.

The Hopkins and Allen Company made a large variety of pistols and revolvers during the rather long existence of the company.

One Bay State Bicycle rifle was shown in the last book. This was made on a small version of the regular falling block system used on the rifles by this company. I have not seen a bicycle rifle made and marked H & A like the Bay State; however, they did make some detachable stock pistols such as is shown on *Plate Numbers 50 & 51.* These photos show one of the Bicycle Rifles, or a detachable shoulder stock pistol, as the H & A catalogues referred to them. The specifications of this piece are:

Name of Piece: Bicycle Rifle
Maker: Hopkins & Allen Mfg. Company

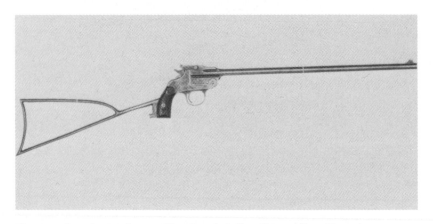

Plate Number 50   Hopkins & Allen Bicycle Rifle. (Photo: Albert Huston).

Serial Number: 1021

Markings on top of barrel: "Hopkins & Allen Arms Co., Norwich, Ct., U.S.A." (Letters are approximately 1/16" tall.) Serial number is on underside of square breech portion of barrel. Also, on underside of frame ahead of breech portion.

Action Type: Tip-up barrel action; also, used on other pistols by this maker.

Caliber: .22 rimfire

Barrel length: 32 3/4"

Sights: Bead on a front blade sight pinned into an integral lug on barrel top. Rear sight is on extreme rear of barrel, adjustable for windage by opposing screws. Also adjustable for elevation by loosening screw on left side breech of barrel and moving sight manually.

Frame: Apparently blued originally.

Barrel tips down for loading when knurled parts on each side of breech are depressed at same time.

Stock: The removeable iron shoulder stock is attached by means of a knurled head, slotted screw at bottom rear of grip. The top of stock, closely fitting the curve of the back strap has a fixed pin which fits into a hole in the back strap one inch above the holding screw at bottom. This screw is pinned into its hole in the stock to prevent loss.

The extractor kicks back into its seat in the barrel after extracting the fired case, like many revolver extractors.

Remarks: This specimen has a very smooth light trigger pull. This one turned up at a farm goods auction near my home and was bought by a friend who attended that sale. The piece was advertised in the sale bill as a "coon hunters special." While not the most scarce Hopkins & Allen Pocket or Bicycle Rifle, this one *is* quite rare.

Plate Number 51   H & A Bicycle Rifle—action opened. (Photo: Albert Huston).

One Hopkins & Allen collector I know has four different H & A versions of the solid frame spur trigger revolvers, about the same as the No. 5 XL, all in .38 caliber and all are smooth bored. All four have wood stocks, some slab, some oval. The barrel lengths range from 12" to 27".

(An old broadside advertising sheet issue by H & A offers: "Blue Jacket and XL Revolvers" in a variety of conformations, but, most are spur or sheath trigger revolvers. There are two single shots, the X-PERT, a sheath trigger derringer-type offered in 22-100 and 30-100 rimfire calibers. The other is the BONNIE BLUE blank cartridge pistol for boys, 22-100 caliber.)

Reproduced here is the rifle section of a 1915 Hopkins & Allen catalogue.

I wish to mention a two-barrel rifle outfit that is similar to that shown in *Boys' Rifles*, except there are no serial numbers on either barrel. The .22 rimfire barrel is marked on top as usual with the H & A name, etc. The other barrel, a .32 caliber, has only the patent dates and does not mention Pat. Appl. For. The action frame is numbered 840 in several places and even the forearm is numbered. It has set trigger, take-down screw, the extractor mechanism for both barrels and changes from rim-to centerfire. The .22 barrel measures 26" and the .32 barrel is 21 7/8" long. The butt plate is hard rubber, shotgun type and is marked *BSA!*

Plate numbers 52 to 62 inclusive, are pages copied from the 1915 Hopkins & Allen Catalogue.

I recently saw at a gun show, a small rolling block system rifle which is a dead ringer for the Model 722 Hopkins & Allen, but without the Hopkins & Allen name.

It was a small light .22 rimfire, marked on the left side of the frame, "ENGERS ROYAL SCOUT" with a full-headress Indian head. A Hopkins & Allen of the same system with this profile of an Indian Head was shown on Page 248, *Boys' Single Shot Rifles*. In this illustration, however, there is no lettering accompanying the head on the left side of the frame. Another example of custom marking practiced some years ago, and still being used, to some extent, today.

No. 722, A Boy's First Rifle

A 3½ lb. 22 Calibre, Take-Down Rifle that is Straight-Shooting, Accurate and Safe. An Ideal First Rifle for Boys.

WHAT boy does not long for a "real rifle" almost from the time he first learns to walk? You can give him an air-gun, but he will never be satisfied with it. Harmless little birds are all he can kill with an air gun, and he instinctively feels that with such a weapon he must either be cruel or have no sport.

But give him a real rifle—one that shoots powder ammunition—and you immediately awaken in him a hundred manly qualities that have been ready to develop. Teach him to be careful with his rifle; teach him to spare the innocent song birds and use his gun only for rabbits, squirrels, hawks, skunks and the target, and you have already started him to develop some of the highest qualities of a man's nature.

Weighs only 3½ lbs. Any boy can handle it.

The main thing in giving your boy a rifle, however, is in being sure that the rifle is safe. It is equipped with a block action—the simplest action that can be devised. This action locks when it is open for loading, and by no chance is it possible for the cartridge to be discharged prematurely while loading. The hammer, when not being fired, rests in the safety notch at half-cock so there is no danger of the hammer being struck and the gun discharged when the boy is not looking for it.

Boys as young as eight years can be safely trusted with the 722 (provided of course, they are taught to use it, and handle it); and any parent who likes to develop manly qualities in his son can feel perfectly safe in presenting "the little fellow" this "Boy's First Rifle."

Price

$3.50

Has All the Up-to-date Features.

A FIRST-CLASS, RELIABLE rifle positively not to be put up at a lower price than this. The No. 722 handles factory loaded rifle cartridge with perfect safety—and shoots the inexpensive rimfire cartridge—short or long. It has plenty of range for the average boy, and is as accurate and straight-shooting, at reasonable range, as the best rifles manufactured.

DESCRIPTION—The No. 722 weighs only three and one-half pounds, has 21½ inch barrel, is 37 inches end to end, and shoots as long as short rimfire cartridges. It handles easily, is simple, light and straight shooting, and positively cannot explode cartridge prematurely when loading.

ACTION—Breech block action, the simplest action made and as safe an action as can be manufactured. The block opens by pulling in lock with thumb not seen in the illustration. When block is pulled back the shell is thrown out, and at the same time the hammer is locked back, preventing it from falling until the gun is ready for use. Cartridge is inserted in chamber, block pushed forward, and the gun is ready for use. (Small cut at bottom explains this action thoroughly.)

BARREL—Is bored out of a solid bar of gun rifle steel, rifled with our patented improved spock twist which gives the greatest accuracy and penetration. Barrel is equipped with knife blade fore sight and sporting rear sight.

STOCK AND FORE END—Made of fine American walnut, carefully seasoned and kiln dried. Will not dry out or crack. Is light, strong and durable. Heavy rubber butt plate—prevents the shoulder slip in quick shooting.

FRAME AND WORKING PARTS—Frame of case hardened steel; working parts, drop-forged and case hardened.

TAKE-DOWN ARRANGEMENT—Screw-Key Pattern. You can take a knife-blade or a penny or a dime and set up this joint solid as a rock (doesn't require a screw driver) and take it down just as easily. The screw tapers at the point, giving it good purchase, and it cuts through the case hardened steel frame, and not through wood as in the case with many cheap rifles. This joint can never wear loose or shoot loose, which is a very important feature. Where the joint is made by a screw set through the wooden stock, wear will make it loosen, and a serious accident may occur.

The No. 722 is a modern, up-to-date rifle with the best safety principles; and a 22 calibre rifle with such quality and features cannot be found elsewhere at a price which approaches ours—$3.50.

Showing How the No. 722 Takes Down, Ejects Shells and Opens for Loading.

NO. 822, FOR BOYS OF 12 TO 16 YEARS

22 Calibre, 4 lbs., 20 in. Barrel 35 ins. from End to End. Quick Working Lever Action, Screw-key Take Down.

THIS rifle, while no safer or more accurate than is the No. 722, in its own range, is quicker in its action, and being longer and heavier, will of course shoot farther. It is designed for the use of boys of from 12 to 16 years, who are able to carry a heavier rifle than the No. 722, and who can be trusted with the quick working Lever Actions.

SHOWING HOW No. 822 TAKES DOWN, EJECTS SHELL AND OPENS FOR LOADING

The No. 822 is also guarded against premature discharge of cartridge while loading, and is equipped with safety locking device for the hammer at half cock.

Any boy, of the proper age, can be trusted with this rifle; and the parent may be sure he will be delighted with its rapid action, great accuracy and extended range. It is an excellent hunting gun for all sorts of small game, and, at the target, will make winning scores every time for the boy who knows how to aim properly.

There may be some question as to whether the little fellow of eight or nine years should be trusted with a gun—it depends on his strength and self reliance, but when a boy gets to be twelve or fourteen years old there is no question but that in every case he should have a rifle. It quickens his sight, develops his arms and legs, gives him control of his nerves, and makes him master of himself, and conscious of his power—all manly qualities.

No. 832

$4.50

Exactly like No. 822 except it is chambered for 32 Cal. short cartridges and shoots the 32 Cal. short only.

Price

$4.50

A Quick Shooting, Quick Handling Rifle that will Delight Young Men.

THE lever action is now considered the highest type of action for single shot sporting rifles; and the action on this rifle is the easiest and quickest working action of the lever type. Being equipped with such an action, the rifle is capable of very rapid shooting for a single shot gun, and as a sporting or target rifle is very desirable.

DESCRIPTION—The No. 822 is 35 inches from end to end, has 20-inch barrel, weighs 4 pounds and shoots 22 calibre, long or short, rimfire cartridges. Because of the lever action it ejects shell and is reloaded very quickly, and its safety features are very desirable.

ACTION—Lever pattern, the working of which is shown in small cut on opposite side of page. A push on the trigger guard lever sends the block on the gun down and throws out the empty shell. Insert a new cartridge, snap up the lever and the gun is ready for use.

BARREL—Bored out of bars of fine rifle steel, rifled with our patented improved extra quick twist which gives the greatest accuracy and penetration.

SIGHTS—Sporting front sight; sporting rear sight.

STOCK AND FORE END—Made of best American walnut, seasoned, kiln dried and matured very carefully, so that there is no danger of splitting or warping. Stock and fore end are light, strong and very durable and of a quality not found on the average low priced gun. Heavy hard rubber butt plate—protects the shoulder in quick shooting.

FRAME AND WORKING PARTS—FRAME fine quality, case hardened steel; WORKING PARTS drop-forged and case hardened steel.

TAKE DOWN ARRANGEMENT—Screw Key pattern. Screw is equipped with ring handle so that no coin or driver is required. Set screw is taper pointed, with taper pointed seat to match—screw therefore sets up very tight and loosens very quickly and easily. Set screw is set through the case hardened frame, and not through wood as is the case with most low priced rifles. Will not loosen from wear or shooting, which is a very desirable point; the wood-seated screw-keys on cheap rifles being liable to bring about serious accidents when they wear loose.

The No. 822 is an exceedingly effective rifle, and, at the price, cannot be matched elsewhere, either in quality or in up-to-date safety and sporting features. It is a superlatively good gun.

FOR BOYS OF 12 TO 16 YEARS

74

No. 922 HOPKINS & ALLEN "JUNIOR"

A RIFLE FOR EXPERTS

MANY years have passed since we first offered the Hopkins & Allen "Junior" Rifle to the public, and it has now regularly taken its place as the recognized standard single shot rifle for the expert, be he man or boy.

The swift lever action and rebounding hammer of the H. & A. Junior are favorite features with expert riflemen, as are the take-down arrangement, good weight and fine balance. But the really supreme feature in the H. & A. Junior—the feature that makes it prized by riflemen—is its unmatched accuracy, due to our patented extra quick twist system of rifling. This feature is exclusive with Hopkins & Allen's rifles and places them in a class which is both apart from and superior to rifles of other makes.

With a Hopkins & Allen "Junior" (plain or fancy stock, round or octagonal barrel) you can be sure of hitting ten times out of ten **exactly where you aim.** Therefore, with this rifle, and practice in aiming and firing, any boy or man can soon put themselves **in a class with the experts.**

The shooting qualities and high character of the workmanship and material used in our Junior Rifle are such as would warrant other factories in asking a higher price for it. But our great buying facilities and our cost-saving system of manufacture enable us to make a fair profit on the "Junior" at the prices we have made for it, and we feel sure that by winning many thousands of new friends through our low prices, we will, in the end, be more than repaid for not placing a high price on the "Junior," thus making long profits out of fewer sales.

Price

$5.50

Shoots 22 Calibre Long or Short, or 22 Calibre, Long Rifle, Cartridge Range 200 Yards.

THE remarkable good fortune that has attended the sale of this rifle since it was first offered the public proves two things; first, that its plainly good quality and fine appearance attract thousands of purchasers who first examine it in stores; and second, that its thousands of purchasers recommend it warmly to other thousands of friends after using it. Thus, and thus only, could the enormous demand we have for the gun be created.

Its grace, fine balance, quick action and beautiful, attractive appearance are what sell it in the stores, and its unusual accuracy, fine handling qualities and exceptional ability to stand hard use, are the things that make its users so enthusiastically recommend the rifle to friends.

Description—The No. 922 "Junior" single shot rifle weighs 4½ lbs., is 38½ inches over all, has 22-inch barrel, has lever action and rebounding hammer, and shoots 22 Calibre long cartridges.

Action—Lever Pattern, the working of which is explained by small cut at bottom of page. Push down the trigger-guard lever and the shell is thrown out, insert new cartridge, snap up the lever and the gun is ready for use. The easiest working quick est action used on a single shot sporting rifle.

Barrel—Round; bored out of round bars of best quality rifle steel, rifled with extra care with our PATENTED improved extra quick twist, which accounts for the "Junior's" wonderful accuracy and great penetration.

Sights—Rear; Rocky Mountain Step, adjustable for 25 to 200 yards range; Front, Sporting Sight.

Stock and Fore End—Made of select walnut, seasoned, kiln dried and matured with great care. Will not warp or crack—is light, strong and durable. Hard rubber butt plate—protects shoulder in quick shooting.

Frame and Working Parts—Frame select, case-hardened steel; working parts drop-forged, case-hardened steel. Hammer rebounds after firing, and locks in safety notch—accidental discharge is therefore provided against.

No. 932

$5.50

32 Calibre. Same as above in every respect, but chambered for .32 cartridge.

Making a Bull's Eye at 200 Yards.

TAKE-DOWN ARRANGEMENT—Screw-key Pattern. Screw provided with ring handle doing away with use of coin or other driver for setting up or loosening. Screw is taper pointed and seated through the case-hardened steel frame. No chance of this joint loosening or shooting off, as in the case with cheap single shot rifles that have the screw-key seated in wood.

The fine, high quality of this gun and its extraordinary power to do hard, bull's-eye shooting put it in a class by itself.

Showing how H. & A. "Junior" Takes Down, Ejects Shell and Opens for Loading.

No. 1922, with Full Octagonal Barrel, $6.00

FOR those who delight in a strong, shapely stock of handsome grain and prefer an octagonal barrel, nothing could be more satisfactory than this rifle. The stock is made of tough, fine-grained walnut, shaped handsomely and very finely finished. The barrel is bored out of solid bars of very fine quality octagon rifle steel, rifled with our patent increase twist; and for shape, handling qualities and accuracy the rifle cannot be excelled.

22 Calibre

4½ pounds

SINGLE SHOT

Length 38½ inches;
Barrel 22 inches.

THE quality of this rifle is the same as No. 2922, but it is finished plainer.

STOCK and **FORE END** are made out of extra select, kiln dried Walnut of choice grain.

BARRELS are bored out of solid bars of octagon rifle steel, rifled with our patented, improved increase twist, which give the greatest range and accuracy.

ACTION is lever type, which works very rapid and easy, and is desirable in every respect.

HAMMER rebounds after firing and never rests on firing pin, making the rifle free from possibility of accident caused by accidental discharge.

BUTT PLATE is heavy, hard rubber giving thorough protection to the shoulder when rapid shooting is required.

No. 1932—32 CALIBRE

Same as above in every respect, but chambered for 32 and shoots 32 calibre cartridge.

PRICE

$6.00

Showing how Rifle is taken down and how lever works in ejecting shell for reloading.

The No. 1922 shoots 22 Calibre short, 22 Calibre long, or 22 Calibre long rifle cartridge with equal ease and accuracy. It is strong, true and very accurate splendid value at our price. Can be supplied with Lyman Sights.

No. 2922
With Fancy Checkered Stock and Fore end, and Full Octagonal Barrel $6.50

A 22 calibre take-down rifle of great beauty and extra fine shooting qualities.

Description

As a single shot rifle this model has no superior on the American market. It is not only extra finished, bringing out the greatest possible beauty in wood and metal, but from a mechanical standpoint is constructed on the most advanced principles used in the manufacture of rifles. The action (Lever Pattern, the working of which can be seen in small rough cut at bottom of page) is the simplest and most improved action in use on a single shot rifle. The lever is hinged in a manner that gives a very strong leverage and makes ejecting and loading quick and easy. The take down (see rough cut at bottom) is a screw-key pattern; but the ring screw is fitted into solid metal and not stock through the wood as is the case with most low priced rifles. The screw can, therefore, never split out or get loose, and the purchaser is sure of as tight a joint after years of use as on the day the rifle was purchased.

STOCK AND FORE END are made from the best extra select kiln dried walnut, the wood used being chosen for its elegant, straight, symmetrical grain. GRIPS are hand checkered in fancy design that gives beauty of appearance, and offers the best hand holds, and the stock is turned off and finished up by the most careful workmen. BARREL is bored out of best octagon bar rifle steel deep rifled with our extra quick twist which furnishes **the best range and penetration.** Sights are: rear Rocky Mountain Step Sight; front, sporting sight—fine enough for any work up to 200 yards, and plain enough for quick, straight shooting. ACTION is Lever Pattern, described above and illustrated in cut at corner of page with **rebounding hammer,** which, upon release of trigger after shooting immediately bounds back, and **locks** entirely free of firing pin, making the rifle an absolute safety. BUTT PLATE is thick hard rubber, giving the shoulder thorough protection where quick shooting is done.

SPECIFICATIONS: No. 2922 shoots either 22 short, long or long rifle cartridges, is 38½ in. over all with barrel 22½ in. which takes down short enough to pack in trunk or suit case or under seat of a wagon or carriage.

THIS model of our 22 calibre single shot "Junior" rifle is designed especially for the discriminating rifle user who likes an extra well finished arm having appearance superior to that found in the plainer models. The Stock and Fore end of No. 2922 are made of extra select seasoned walnut, only the attractive grains being selected from stock for this particular pattern. The grips are checkered by hand in a fancy design that offers both an excellent handhold and an added fineness to the rifle's appearance. The frame is case hardened with especial care, so that the fine, blue tone brought out by the tempering is blended richly with the browns and greys, making an extremely handsome pattern. The finish, aligning and assembling are the best that can be produced; and the rifle is in every way up to the top notch of modern American workmanship.

Whether the purchaser be one who is securing his first rifle, or a man who has used small rifles for many years and is well versed in rifle values, the No. 2922 is amply qualified to give more than usual satisfaction. Not only does it shoot 22 long or short or long rifle, rimfire cartridges with extreme accuracy and penetrating force, balance beautifully and handle in a manner that gives great confidence to the shooter, but for the price it has a beauty that makes it desirable even apart from its splendid qualifications for expert shooting.

Probably no one of our guns is a better purchase than another from a value standpoint, as we try to put the limit of value into every firearm of our manufacture; but with the increase on margin to work on, we can assure to all purchasers of the No. 2922 a rifle that in appearance, finish and shooting qualities is more than desirable at our price, and, for those who desire such a gun, is even more desirable than our Junior No. 922.

No. 2932—$6.50

32 Calibre

Same as above in every respect but chambered for 32 calibre cartridge

At $6.50 this Rifle is among the best bargains we offer, which means that its equal cannot be found elsewhere at like low price. We guarantee this Gun to shoot true to aim at any distance to which the ammunition can be expected to accurately carry.

Any standard rimfire ammunition can be used; and this includes factory-loaded smokeless powder cartridges.

This rifle can be fitted with Lyman Sights if so desired.

Showing how Nos. 2922 and 1922 take down and working of lever to eject shell

27

No. 3922, H. & A.
CELEBRATED SCHUETZEN RIFLE
22 CALIBRE, TAKE DOWN, FULL OCTAGON BARREL FOR FINE TARGET WORK

Price

$12.⁰⁰

22 Calibre for 22 short, long and long Rifle Cartridge. Full octagon barrel.

THE quality of material, and the grade of workmanship put into these Schuetzen rifles are the best that our factory can produce — and as we manufacture in large quantities and employ the best machinery and labor that can be obtained, this means that those who buy Schuetzen rifles of our manufacture are assured quality and rifle value that other factories could not possibly produce at an equal price.

DESCRIPTION—No. 3922 Schuetzen is a 22 Calibre rifle of great beauty, splendid balance and a reputation for fine shooting in the short and extreme 22 Calibre ranges. It is 41 inches long, with 26 inch barrel and weighs 5½ pounds. Shoots 22 Calibre short, 22 Calibre long and 22 Calibre long rifle nitro or black powder cartridges.

BARREL—Is made of the finest rifle steel bored from solid octagon bars and rifled with extreme care by the best workmen with our **patented**, improved extra quick twist, which perfects the trajectory and increases the range and penetration.

SIGHTS—Sporting fore sight and Rocky Mountain Step rear sight adjusted for from 25 to 200 yards.

ACTION—Lever type, same as used on our "Junior" 22 Calibre rifles—the best and quickest action known for target or sporting rifle. Push down the lever—out flies the shell; insert a new cartridge, snap up the lever and your gun is ready to fire again. Hammer rebounds **after firing, and cannot touch the cartridge except when you cock and fire.** Trigger pull is very light.

STOCK AND FORE END—Made of extra select English Walnut of especially attractive grain—seasoned, kiln-dried and matured with extra care. Will not warp or crack—beautifully shaped, fine to handle, helps the gun roll up high scores. Stock and fore end are handsomely hand checkered in a design that is not only beautiful but easy and firm to the grip. **Nickel finished Schuetzen butt plate: conforms to shape of shoulder and gives steady aim.**

FRAME AND WORKING PARTS—Frame of best quality **tough,** case hardened steel, of beautiful pattern; working parts **drop-forged,** case hardened steel of best quality.

THE Hopkins & Allen Schuetzen Rifles are now so well known among expert riflemen in every part of the world that extended comment regarding them seems almost unnecessary. No rifle of 22 or 25-20 Calibre is capable of making higher scores than the H. & A. Schuetzens,—and there are few rifles in these Calibres that can even compete with them. Special care is taken with the rifling, and our famous **patented** increase twist being used in these arms, the purchaser is assured the greatest accuracy in all ranges and the highest amount of penetration. Many Schuetzen Rifle Clubs in various parts of the country are using the Hopkins & Allen Schuetzens for the lighter class of target work, and the reports we have from them are invariably gratifying. There are Schuetzen rifles sold for a fancier price than ours and Schuetzens with fine, expensive outside plating and elaborate hand engraving. But it is seldom indeed that the owner of one of these rifles is able to report a higher score than the owners of the old, reliable Hopkins & Allen Schuetzens—and never can they report an evener run of **good** scores.

Our Schuetzen Rifles are noted for their good quality, and plain, desirable finish. Such a gun is easier to take care of, and less liable to rust, gum or corrode, from use and weather. These qualities, with their reputation for uniform high grade shooting month after month, have endeared the Hopkins & Allen Schuetzens to thousands of riflemen, and have compelled hundreds of former admirers of the fancy type of Schuetzen to give them preference.

The demand for these guns is increasing year after year, and it will increase still further when the great merits of the rifles become more widely known through actual experience.

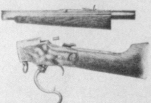

Showing how Gun Takes Down and how Lever Works in Ejecting Shell for Reloading.

This is a 22 Calibre target and sporting rifle of exceptionally fine quality, and of very beautiful appearance. It will abundantly please every purchaser.

No. 3925, 25-20 SCHUETZEN RIFLE
With or Without Lyman Sights—Full Octagon Barrel

Exact Size of 25-20 Cartridge

THIS rifle is turned out specially to please those who desire a rifle of unusual penetrating power and accuracy. It is not only a long range target gun that cannot be excelled for accuracy, but aside from its target uses, is a gun that is capable of killing almost any kind of game at long range. Deer, Antelope, Wolves, Coyotes, Cougars, etc., may be brought down with this gun; and for the turkey shoot there is no better gun in the market. Without Lyman sights the rifle is remarkable for its accuracy at all the ranges—short and long; and with the Lyman sights the accuracy of the gun becomes minute to a degree that excites comment and admiration.

On the farm the gun also is very valuable. You can pick a hawk or crow from a tree almost as far as you can see, and can bring down a fox or skunk at a surprising distance. Beeves, hogs and sheep may be also killed with it; and at the turkey shoot the farmer who owns a 25-20 Schuetzen can walk off with the trophy as often as he pleases. Wild turkeys, which furnish very difficult shooting, grouse, woodcock, etc., may be killed with it, and in localities where there are frequent rifle contests, a No. 3925 Schuetzen owner can get the best of the prizes.

The finish of the gun, its material and the fine, expert way in which it is put together are points which excite favorable comment from all who see it. It is in every way a topnotch firearm—a pleasure giver and a trophy winner.

Price with Lyman Sights

$19.50

without Lyman Sights

$15.00

THE wood and metal used in this gun are of the finest quality, and the workmanship used in constructing it is of the best that the American firearms field can produce. From butt to muzzle there is not an ounce of material or one step in construction that is not of the very best quality, and the finished arm is a product of grace, fine balance, and great beauty.

Description—The 3925-25-20 Schuetzen is patterned after the famous Hopkins & Allen 22 Calibre, No. 3922 Schuetzen, and has the same fine shooting qualities, but is made heavier in stock and barrel to take care of the heavier ammunition. The No. 3925 Schuetzen weighs 7 lbs. instead of 5 lbs., is 41 inches long, has 26 inch barrel.

Barrel—Made of finest quality select rifle steel, bored out of solid octagon bars, and rifled with our **patented** extra quick twist, which lessens the trajectory and gives the greatest range and penetration obtainable.

Sights—On the $19.50 Gun, the famous Lyman Patent Combination Rear Sight with cup disc, and Lyman's Patent Combination Ivory Front Sight—this gun also has Rocky Mountain Step, Rear Sight in addition. On the $15.00 Gun, Rocky Mountain Adjustable Step, Rear Sight and Sporting Front Sight only.

Action—The superb Lever type, used on our 22 Calibre Schuetzen and on our 22 Calibre "Juniors." No better action can be found for a sporting or target rifle.

Stock and Fore End—Of extra select English walnut, chosen for its beautiful grain and freedom from blemish—seasoned; kiln-dried and matured with extreme care. Machine turned, hand finished and checkered. A light, powerful stock and fore end that handle supremely well, balance evenly and add to the gun's accuracy. Checkering designs are both beautiful and designed to give firm, easy handhold in every kind of weather. Stock is equipped with nickeled Schuetzen butt plate, which conforms perfectly to shape of shoulder, and insures a steady aim.

Frame and Working Parts—Frame of extra fine quality **case hardened** steel, working parts **drop-forged** and case hardened.

With or without the Lyman sights, this gun is a model of beauty, accuracy and shooting power, but for very fine shooting, especially at long range, we would say that the Lyman sights easily add 50% to the gun's efficiency.

Showing how Gun Takes Down and how Lever Works in Ejecting Shell

No. 5022—JUNIOR REPEATING RIFLE

With Fancy Hand Checkered Stock and Fore End

Exact Size of Ammunition
22 Short, 22 Long and
22 Long Rifle

Price

$12.00

22 Calibre — 16 Shots

THIS gun is especially designed for those who like extra fine appearance in a repeating rifle. It has all the features of the 88.75 repeating rifle shown on page opposite — Military Bolt Action, side ejection, positive safety device, promiscuous magazine feed, etc., but is made of finer materials and greater care is used to secure that exquisite look so much desired by a certain class of rifle users; every part of the gun and every inch of the stock and barrel is gone over with greatest care in order to bring out the greatest possible grace and give the most perfect alignment and best balance to the finished arm.

The result is a rifle that will please the most exacting sportsman. The illustration, though made from a photograph, does only partial justice to the gun. Some idea of its appearance is given, but to appreciate the rich, beautiful grain, and the exquisite color and appearance of stock and fore end, and the brilliant finish of barrel and parts, you would have to see the rifle itself.

There are few 22 calibre rifles, even the highest priced kind, that are as beautiful in finish and appearance, or which have more graceful lines.

We offer in the No. 5022 a rifle of the highest and most luxurious type, and the owner of it can be sure of exciting admiration everywhere, and in any company.

Although to be able to offer such a rifle as the plain Junior Repeater at $8.75 is an achievement we are proud of, we are equally pleased at the fact that we are able to offer such an exclusive rifle as the No. 5022 at $12. The rifle is really worth a much higher price.

THE No. 5022 Junior Repeater has the same general features as the 88.75 Junior Repeater shown on the opposite page, but is finished with greater attention to detail and with greater regard for securing an exceptionally elegant appearance.

DESCRIPTION — All the materials are of select grade, and the finishing is done by the best men and the finest machinery in our factory. The gun is 38½ inches long, has barrel 22 inches long, and weighs 5½ lbs. — same weight and specifications as the 88.75 plain Junior Repeater. It also shoots 22 short, 22 long or 22 long rifle cartridges without change of carrier, and feeds short, long and long rifle cartridges mixed together, if desired.

Stock and Fore End — Made of extra fine imported English walnut, seasoned, kiln-dried and matured with great care — selected only from wood having a beautiful, close, curled grain (as is shown by the illustration), which insures strength and adds to the rifle's luxurious appearance. Stock and fore end are beautifully checkered by hand (as shown in cut) in a pattern that is specially graceful and specially designed to give a firm grip and steady aim. Stock is equipped with fine tempered steel butt plate which effectually protects it, setting well to the shoulder, holding the gun very steady.

Barrel — Made from especially selected bars of fine rifle steel, specially finished and rifled with our PATENTED improved extra quick twist which gives the best range and highest penetration known.

Sights — Rocky Mountain Step rear sight, adjusted for from 15 to 200 yards and opening front sight. The sights are plain, easy and accurate, coarse enough for quick, accurate work in the short ranges, and fine enough for bull's eye shooting at long range.

Action — Is the Superb Military Bolt pattern which has proven so popular on our 88.75 plain Junior Repeater. This action is the best known for a repeating rifle — the kind used by leading nations for their regulation military guns. This action EJECTS AT THE SIDE the fired shell, thus guarded from flying shells and the barrel and mechanism of the gun is protected from rain, sleet, sand and weather. The action is also equipped with A POSITIVE SAFETY device, eliminating danger from premature discharge of the cartridge.

Magazine — Is the simplest and safest used on a repeating rifle. It holds 11 22 short and 16 22 long rifle cartridges, and feeds 22 short, long and long rifle cartridges mixed together, if desired. It is the only magazine that will eject cartridges after loading without having to work them out one by one through the ejector. This is an excellent feature, as one will often have had a dozen cartridges or so left in the magazine which he will at the end of a shoot wish to remove before putting the rifle away or packing it.

Take-Down — Screw key pattern, with taper-pointed set screw that can be set so very tight or loosened with a small blade or small tool. Screw is seated in the steel breech of the rifle and not up through the wood as is often the case with other repeaters. This point cannot loosen or shoot off as the wood shrinks and can do.

The No. 5022 will keep its beautiful appearance for years, and will be found the straightest and hardest shooting 22 calibre repeating rifle manufactured.

LYMAN COMBINATION PEEP and GLOBE SIGHTS

Supplied on this rifle (No. 5022) as well as on the No. 4922 and American Military Rifles at $3.50 extra.

No. 2044, Baby Shotgun

44 CALIBRE
FOR TAXIDERMISTS
BOYS AND WOMEN

THIS is the kind of shotgun used by bird collectors for taking small plumage and game birds without tearing the body.

It is also a good first shotgun for the small boys and for the use of women. Every woman should learn how to handle a gun, even if she does not learn how to use a revolver; and the No. 2044 is the lightest and most desirable shotgun made for this purpose. It shoots only a few shot in a small 44 calibre cartridge, and is very light and easily handled; but it is sufficient to drive off a tramp or a ruffian and rid the neighborhood of small feathered pests such as English sparrows or of rats, etc. Besides, it is a splendid little gun for light target practice.

It will furnish a great deal of entertainment (at a very slight cost for ammunition) in the country home where a safe range for such a gun is found easily near the house and where guests, especially ladies and young people, may be amused shooting. Among taxidermists the No. 2044 is too well known to require description.

Price

$9.00

**5 lbs.
Breech
Loading
Lever Action.**

THE quality of the No. 2044 Baby Shotgun is very superior. It has all the good features of our rifles —lever action, rebounding hammer, screw key, take down, etc., and is very light, strong and well balanced. It weighs only 5 lbs. and is but 40 inches long from end to end—just a nice length to handle. The barrel is but 20 inches, so that, when taken down, the gun will easily go into a trunk or dress suit case.

DESCRIPTION:

STOCK
Fine beautifully grained walnut with graceful pistol grip, offering a good hand hold—butt plate, hard rubber.

BARREL
Fine quality blued steel, bored perfectly, very accurate.

FRAME
Very fine, case hardened steel. Light and tough. Graceful shape, beautiful in appearance.

ACTION
Fast working, safety lever. Pattern same as our rifles. Pushing down trigger guard opens breech and throws out shell; insert new cartridge, snap up lever and gun is loaded. This action is simple, safe, and very quick.

TAKE-DOWN
Screw Key pattern—takes down and puts together in 10 to 15 seconds. Screw sets in solid metal, taper cell and point. Cannot pull out or work loose. Sets up very tight.

HAMMER
Rebounds. Never touches cartridge except when gun is fired.

Mechanism of H. & A. Baby Shotgun—Showing screw-key inserted and barrel taken down; also the first trigger-guard open to throw out the shell.

There is no other 44 Calibre Shotgun that offers the advantages of this one, especially at the price.

We can guarantee it for accuracy, fine quality, good balance and durability.

IV

A Miscellaneous Assortment

In Chapter VI, Page 173 of *Boys' Single Shot Rifles*, I mentioned that I had not then seen a Quackenbush Model 5 combination rifle with means to extract the fired .22 rimfire case.

I am now able to show this improvement and it is displayed on *Plate Number 63.* A description of the rifle follows:

Name of rifle: Quackenbush.

Model: Combination rifle Number 5.

Markings: On top tang: "H. M. Quackenbush, Herkimer, N.Y., U.S.A." in one line.

Other Markings: None, except serial number 2477.

Action type: Break open.

Caliber: .22 Short rimfire, and air rifle shot or dart.

Barrel length: 22 inches.

Butt plate: Rifle butt plate.

Sights: Screw-in blade front, open rear.

Frame: Blued.

Remarks: In addition to having the extractor shown, this rifle doesn't have the groove in the right side of the breech block (Plate 67, Figures A & B and Plate 68, *Boys' Rifles*). This groove may have been for using an instrument to remove the washer or firing pin. This rifle also has a spring loaded pin with a retaining screw between the barrel latch studs on top of the breech block to hold the firing pin in by friction.

Plate Number 63   Model 5 Quackenbush—breech open. (Photo: Jack C. Faglie).

This chapter, called "Miscellaneous," contains additional information on models previously discussed in *Boys' Rifles* such as the above on the Model 5 Quackenbush. It will also mention some oddball rifles which have come to light since the last book was compiled. In most instances, regarding these pieces, no photo will be shown as their scarcity doesn't warrant it.

An exception to that statement is the Powell & Son rifle illustrated on *Plate Numbers 64 and 65* and which shows the rifle opened and closed.

This same rifle system was also shown on an old letterhead as or *Plate Number 66.*

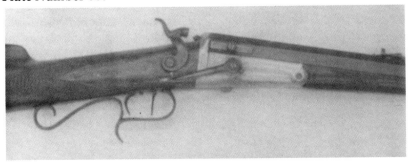

Plate Number 64   Powell & Son breechloading rifle. (Photo: **Richard Donaldson**).

Plate Number 65   Powell & Son breechloader—action open.
(Photo: **Richard Donaldson**).

Plate Number 66 Powell & Son stationery using the breechloading rifle for letterhead.

The actual rifle shown on *Plate Number 64* is a .44 caliber taking a shell about 1-5/8″ long.

Jerry Crozier also reports having examined one of these Powell & Son rifles which had a .38-55 E. Remington & Son barrel. This was possibly rebarreled at one time; however, both the action and barrel are marked with Roman numerals "VIIII." Weight of this particular rifle was 9 lbs.

I saw a "Chas. C. Coleman—Patented May 13, 1902" single shot rifle at an Ohio Gun Show. A ring trigger, by means of a forward motion, releases a falling breech block. All the mechanism is contained in this breech block. This specimen, apparently in .38 rimfire, is the only one I have observed to date.

Next is a German-made rifle, the WIERHAUCH. This rifle was originally made in a .22 centerfire caliber and has been rebarreled to .357 Magnum by its present owner. This is a falling block system.

C. Patt

The C. Patt rifles turn up occasionally. You will recall he was a gunsmith located in Alma, Wisconsin. He imported actions from Switzerland and most seem to have been of the Martini system. Two of his barreling jobs used No. 4 Winchester barrels. The actions were marked "C. PATT, ALMA, WIS." and were blued finish. They seem to be found mainly in Wisconsin and Minnesota. Several have turned up in that region.

Another Patt-Martini, now in the Northwest, was bought by the present owner in Minnesota. This rifle has a No. 4 part-octagon Winchester .32-40 barrel on it. However, it may have been originally barreled for the .40-50 B.N. Sharps cartridge as it is marked on the left side of the receiver, ".40-50, C. Patt, Alma, Wis." There were also empty cases in the .40-50 B.N. size, as well as loading tools for this caliber with the rifle when obtained by its owner. This rifle has a Scheutzen lever and a Swiss buttstock with a cheek piece. A large

68

disc receiver sight sits atop the rear of the Martini action. This action has a rather long upper tang. Another Patt was reported as being in caliber .44-40.

An odd-appearing, side lever rifle, of which I have photos but have not examined personally, is one which the present owner believes to be an experimental pilot or pre-production model of a single shot Bullard. He bases this belief upon the facts it has what appears to be the same frame as later under-lever operated Bullards with the necessary change to be operated by a side lever. The forend wood extends back into the action 3/4" to take up the space where the under lever would be. The caliber is .38-45 Bullard and the plain stock has the Bullard "Turkey" butt plate. There are no markings on the rifle.

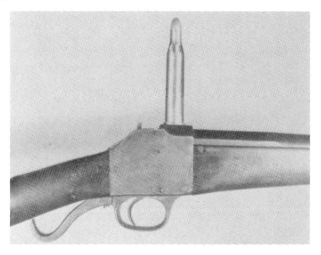

Plate Number 67   An unknown maker's rifle with the cartridge developed for it by Harold Armstrong.

Plate Number 67 shows an unknown maker's efforts in the single shot field. This shows the action closed and *Plate Number 68* pictures it opened to receive the cartridge. This rifle was found by the late Harold Armstrong, who gathered it up, took it home and after casting the chamber, turned up the steel cartridge shown on top of the receiver ring which fits this chamber.

Diameter under head	.773
Diameter of rim	.891
Diameter at mouth	.472
Rim thickness	.0781
Diameter of bullet	.453
Diameter case at shoulder	.745
Length under head to start of shoulder	2-9/16"
Length of neck	1/2"
Case length overall	3-9/16"

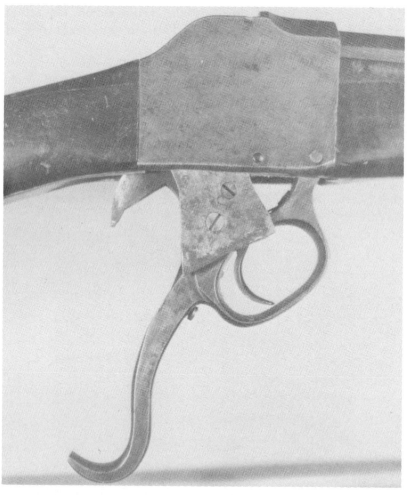

Plate Number 68   An unknown maker's rifle shown with breech open.

(Photo: P. H. Armstrong).

This action has a quite massive frame 2 9/16″ deep at barrel housing. The frame thickness is 1 15/32″. The octagon part of the barrel is 1 3/16″ across the flats and it is 27/32″ diameter at the muzzle, 25¾″ long overall with the octagon part quite short, 4-5/8″ long. It has no sights nor sight slots. The buttstock is secured to long tangs by means of a top tang screw threaded into the lower tang. Forearm is held by means of one screw into a block dovetailed into the bottom of barrel. Plain walnut stocks. Iron butt plate marked on top lip "CS" but no other markings. The hammer must be in a safety notch (first notch) for breech to open. There are also a half cock and a full cock notch on the hammer. Hammer will fall from any of the three notches when trigger is pulled.

Barber and Lefever

The Barber and Lefever rifle. Two of these single shot rifles are accounted for so far. The first is serial numbered 282 and resembles a neat single barrel shotgun. The small outside hammer is on the right side and strikes the angled firing pin to fire the .44-60 cartridge. It opens with a system similar to the Wurfflein but the thumb operated lever is pushed, rather than pulled, to open the barrel. It has both a tang sight and an open barrel sight. The front sight is hooded and has a long dovetail for windage adjustment. The 30-inch barrel is part octagon, part round. The pistol grip stock and forearm are both checkered. *Plate Numbers 69 and 70.*

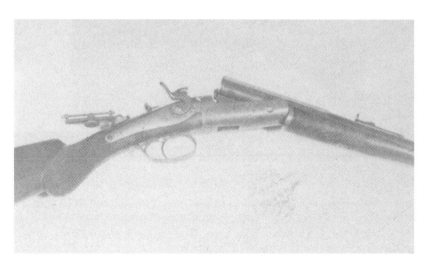

Plate Numbers 69 & 70   Barber & Lefever Single Shot .44-60, full view and breech section open. (Photos: Leo Cook).

The second rifle, number 301, is a rather heavy match or target rifle. It has a tapered 33½″ part octagon, part round barrel, caliber .45-70. Pistol grip stock and forend are both checkered. Weight 11 pounds, 50″ long overall, and has an original two-pronged Scheutzen butt plate. The top prong is detachable and serves double duty as the butt plate top holding screw. It has the same top barrel releasing device as the former rifle described. *Plate numbers 71 and 72.*

The following brief biographical notes on Daniel Lefever are from Mr. H. J. Swinney, director of The Margaret Strong Woodbury Museum at Rochester, New York.

Daniel Lefever was born in 1835, and began his long career in the gun business when he was apprenticed, probably in Canandaiqua, New York, about 1850 or 1851. He set up his own shop there about 1859, and took J. A. Ellis into partnership in 1862. Ellis bought the shop out in 1867, and by 1870 Lefever was in Auburn, New York, experimenting with breechloading shotguns. By 1872 he had joined F. S. Dangerfield, who had a machine shop and foundry. The patent for the early Lefever shotgun action was granted (curiously) to Dangerfield Sept. 3, 1872, and assigned to both Lefever and Dangerfield. Although the correct firm name was F. S. Dangerfield & Co., guns are known marked "Dangerfield & Lefever."

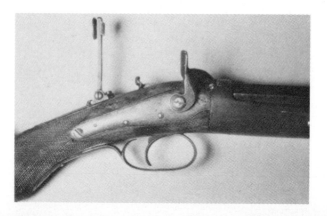

Plate Numbers 71 & 72   Barber & Lefever heavy match rifle in .45-70.

(Photos: A. C. Atterbury).

A specimen of the Dangerfield & Lefever is shown on *Plate Number 73*. The specifications of this combination rifle-shotgun are as follows:

Name of rifle: Dangerfield & Lefever.

Model: Two barrel; rifle and shotgun barrels.

Maker: Dangerfield & Lefever.

Serial Number: "2" marked on side of barrel lug.

Marked on top flat of barrel: Dangerfield & Lefever, Auburn, New York.

On bottom of barrel lug: Pat'd. Sept. 3, 1872.

Action type: Tip-up barrel, released by knurled bar on upper tang sliding forward.

Caliber: Rifle barrel, .58 Dangerfield centerfire; shotgun barrel, 12 gauge.

Barrel length; rifle 30 inches; shotgun barrel 34 inches.

Remarks: The patent on this action was registered to Francis S. Dangerfield, Auburn, New York. He subsequently assigned the same to himself and Daniel M. Lefever.

The shotgun barrel has the same markings as the rifle barrel and has its own case-hardened metal forend.

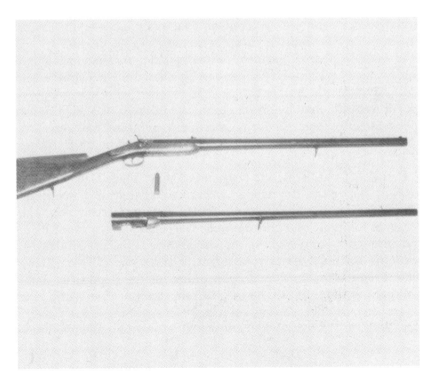

Plate Number 73   Dangerfield & Lefever combination rifle-shotgun in .58 caliber and 12 gauge. (Photo: David Cox Collection).

The .58 Dangerfield cartridge is also pictured with the rifle and shotgun barrels. The dimensions of this cartridge are: Length overall 2.782 inches. The folded head case is 2.112 inches long with a diameter of .637 inches. The primer is slightly recessed, of the brass Berdan type and is typical "large rifle" in size. The rim has a diameter of .706 inches and a thickness of .066 inches. Bullet diameter is .585 inches.

Gardner (*Small Arms Makers*, Col. Robert Gardner, Crown Publishers 1963, New York) lists the following entry:

Dangerfield F.S. & Co. Gunmakers of Auburn, N.Y. 1870-1874, probably Francis S. Dangerfield, Dangerfield, Francis S., Auburn, N.Y., Patented breech loading firearms, September 3, 1872. (Number 130,984) assigned to himself and Daniel M. Lefever.

About 1874, Lefever moved to Syracuse, and soon became associated with Lorenzo Barber. Beginning in 1875, the company advertised itself as "L. Barber & Co. Sole manufacturers of Lefever's Patent Improved Breech-Loading Shot Guns and Rifles. Muzzle Loaders altered to Breech Loaders. No. 51 Clinton St., Syracuse, N.Y." Despite the firm name in the ad, I have inspected several guns clearly stamped "Barber & Lefever/Syracuse, N.Y." One of these had either been converted from, or entirely rebuilt from, a Greener muzzleloader, and was marked on the water table of the frame "Lefever/PAT'D/ Sept. 3, 1872./ Syracuse/N.Y." on the rib.

In April 1876, ads appeared in *Forest and Stream* announcing that Nichols and Lefever of Syracuse had purchased the machinery and tools "of the late L. Barber & Co.," and that they were now prepared to fill orders. But by 1879, John A. Nichols was advertising independently, and the first entry in a Syracuse city directory appeared for "Daniel M. Lefever, gun manufacturer, 78 E. Water St."

Daniel Lefever, known to his generation as "Uncle Dan" went on making fine guns through a succession of confusing corporate reorganizations until his death in 1906 in Bowling Green, Ohio. The Syracuse company that bore his name was sold to Ithaca about 1915, and the gun converted to an inexpensive Ithaca-type double, retaining the old Lefever rotary bolt. At least one of Uncle Dan's sons, Frank Lefever, wound up working for the Remington Arms Company in Ilion; formed his own custom gun firm after World War II; and died in 1950. The custom firm is still operating in Lee Center, New York.

C. E. Overbaugh

Another lever-actuated, crossbolt (similar to a shotgun) single shot rifle is the Overbaugh. One specimen of this unusual rifle is marked on the barrel, "C. E. OVERBAUGH NEW YORK," and on the lock "C. E. OVERBAUGH." The barrel is about a No. 4 weight caliber .38-40 Remington (according to a chamber cast), pistol gripped buttstock and forend are checkered. The buttstock has a hard rubber Sharps type butt plate. The side-hammer lock plate is detached in the English manner. The gun is not an English product, evidently, as there are no British proof marks. The serial number is 1034.

It is reported that C. E. Overbaugh worked for Sharps and went into business for himself when Sharps terminated business. Sawyer mentions a New York maker of the same name, with no initials, as a maker of single shot rifles in the 1885 period, but with a rolling block system action. Perhaps there are other Overbaughs around differing from this one described here?

I show one Overbaugh rifle on *Plate Number 74.*

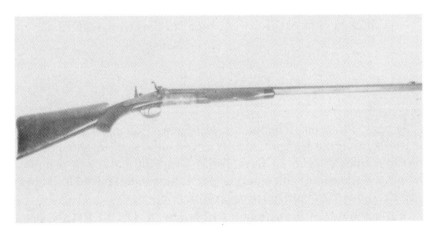

Plate Number 74   C. E. Overbaugh Rifle in .38-40 caliber.
(Photo: David Cox Collection).

This is a finely made tip-up rifle which is described below:
Name of rifle: Overbaugh.
Model: Target.
Maker: C. E. Overbaugh.
Serial Number: 1038 on bottom of barrel, receiver rail and inside of metal forend fitting.
Marked on top flat of barrel: C. E. Overbaugh, New York.
On lock plate: C. E. Overbaugh.

Initials "E.G." stamped on receiver rail. The number "2" also stamped on receiver rail and bottom of barrel.

Action type: Side hammer tip-up with back action lock and horizontal operating tang lever.

Sights: Wind Gauge adjustment front blade and an integral micrometer tang sight. No rear barrel slot.

Remarks: Case-hardened frame, hammer and lock as well as blued trigger guard and top tang lever are scroll engraved. Forend tip and pistol grip cap are of horn. The horn butt plate is typical Sharps pattern with its scroll logo. The deluxe stock has a check piece with fine checkering. The checkered forend has engraved metal fittings and the recessed lever release found in early, better grade shotguns. This piece is quite a splendid rifle. There is no way of knowing if he made or merely purchased the back action lock. The number "2" that is stamped on the receiver rail and bottom of the barrel is more like a "Frame weight" or assembly number, though I have no explanation for the apparent four-digit serial number. It seems to me that the number which appears to be a serial number is way too high in view of the scarcity today of the Overbaugh rifle.

A. Dickerman

Strong Firearms Company of New Haven, Connecticut, manufactured the Dickerman rifle as you will recall. A photo of one of these rifles appears in *Boys' Rifles.* The rifle I want to mention now is a Dickerman with a part octagon, part round barrel in caliber .38-55. It has a shotgun buttstock, pistol gripped.

Across the side of the action in a ribbon is "A. DICKERMAN, Pat. Aug. 4, 1885." Under the forearm is the number "1322R."

I have had several odd-ball, probably one of a kind, rifles brought to my attention in the years since *Volume Three, Boys' Single Shot Rifles,* was published. These have been various systems and none have been marked with makers' names, serial number, etc. Some bear a resemblance to existing known makers' products and in some cases the present owners feel they are pilot or inventors pre-production models of rifles we know about.

If I could have obtained good photos or drawings of these together with careful descriptions, I would have considered them for inclusion in this chapter. However, in almost all cases I have been able to get only sketchy details or poor photos of them so am forced to omit them. I am sorry about this, but when I cannot get the authenticated details of any piece, I have no other choice. I thank the men who have called these to my attention and it is unfortunate that proper photos, etc. could not be obtained, as some of the actions displayed on these are intriguing to me and would be to others, too.

Alexander Henry

An interesting side hammer Alexander Henry rifle is shown on *Plate Numbers 75-76-77*. This is a takedown-barrel rifle, the first we have been able to report on. This plate shows the under side of the rifle with the forearm takedown lever at front end of the wood. The rifle is owned by Joel Tavormina who contacted the presently surviving successor of Alexander Henry, John Dickson & Son of Glasgow, Scotland. Their records show this rifle was "Specially produced in July 1887 for a Sir R. Sutton as a best grade .450 Single Breechloading Rifle with 28-inch detachable barrel, falling block action, right hand lock, lever forend, weight 7 lbs. 13 ozs.". The rifle is chambered for the .450 3¼″ cartridge, a black powder Express cartridge used for large game during this period.

In taking down this rifle, the lever on the forend is turned to the side and the forend is thus removed. Next, a lever mounted on the receiver extension is turned 90° downward, this allows the barrel to be rotated to the left. The lug is on the bottom of the receiver extension, and after under-lever of the rifle is pushed forward to free the horseshoe-shaped ejector from the barrel breech, the barrel may be turned to the left and removed.

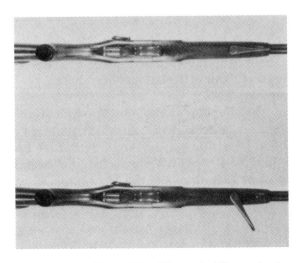

Plate Number 75   Alexander Henry Rifle. (Photos: Joel Tavormina.)

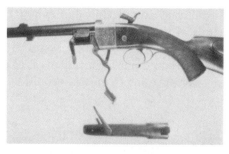

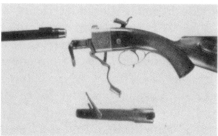

Plate Numbers 76 & 77 Successive stages of take-down for Alexander Henry Rifle.

There are no threads or other milled parts to engage the barrel to the receiver; nor are there cams or tightening devices. The barrel rotating its lug into the receiver extension recess and the horseshoe ejector are all that are used to stabilize barrel to frame. The main specifications of the rifle are:

Barrel: Round 28" long with Henry rifling. Caliber .450 — 3¼" proved for 52 grain light Cordite load, Birmingham.

Action: Engraved and color case-hardened. Barrel is blued a deep blue-black.

Stock: Oil finished French walnut with cheekpiece and rubber recoil pad.

Sights: A fore-sight of a small British type bead.

Rear sight is a 100-yard stationary leaf and a 200-yard folding leaf, both with platinum line inlays.

Serial number: 6085.

At one of the Dayton shows of the Ohio Gun Collectors Association, I saw a side hammer rifle which appeared identical to the Henry rifles. This rifle was marked "HORSLEY PATENTEE" and also "M. W. LANG, MAKER" on the barrel. A beautifully made piece, falling block (identical?? to the Henry), in .40 caliber. This maker also possibly fabricated the opposing screw windage front sight and the vernier rear tang sight, as they are different from any I have observed on any British-made rifles. This one was made by THOMAS HORSLEY & SON, OF YORK. This is a left-hand, outside hammer piece.

German Zimmerstutzen Rifle.

Plate Number 78 illustrates three different German parlor, saloon or Zimmerstutzen rifles.

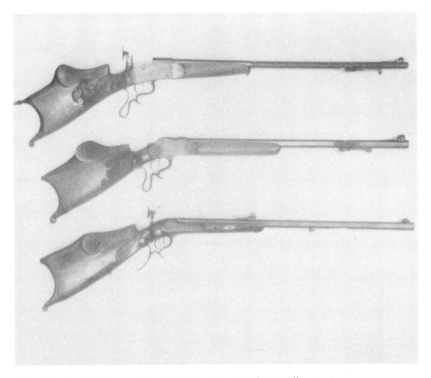

Plate Number 78 German Parlor Rifles. (Photo: John R. Allington).

The top rifle on *Plate Number 78* is marked "A SCHURK-MUNCHEN." The rifled section of the barrel is 7" long and has a groove diameter of .182. Overall length is 47" and weight is 10½ lbs. The unmarked rifle in center of the plate is 43" overall, 7½" of rifled barrel and with a groove diameter of .175 and also weighs 10½ lbs.

The lower rifle is unmarked, weighs 8¼ lbs. and has an overall length of 42" with a 7½" barrel. This rifle was originally 4 mm caliber, with some sort of removeable breech mechanism that drops out of an opening in the bottom of barrel. Since this mechanism was lost and the bore was gone, the present owner had the barrel lined to .22 rimfire. It shoots C B caps well. One other rifle with the same type of breech mechanism, also with this part missing, has been seen. It is believed it was designed for fixed ammunition which is just the same as the separate ball and cap, only the ball is shoved into the cap.

Plate Number 79 shows a close-up of the mechanism on the middle rifle pictured. The top rifle has a similar mechanism.

Plate Number 80 illustrates another view with the 4 mm ball and the primed case lying on the flat of the barrel. (Indicated by the arrow on the photo.)

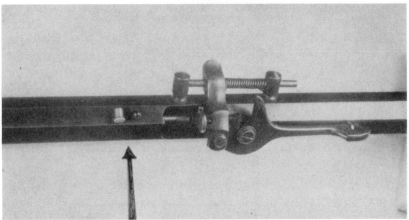

Plate Numbers 79 & 80   Close-up of firing mechanism of middle rifle on Plate 78. Lower Photo shows primed case and 4mm ball, as indicated by arrow.

These rifles are nominally 4 mm caliber but the bores differ and 4 mm balls are available in a number of different sizes to fit. By comparing *Plate Numbers 79 and 80* you may see how these are loaded. The cup goes toward the breech and the ball is put into the front of the swing-out chamber. There is a septum between the cap and ball and when the lever closes the mechanism, the ball is shoved up into the rifling. The firing pin extends all the way up to the barrel and is shown in the fallen position in *Plate Number 80*, and cocked in *Plate Number 79.*

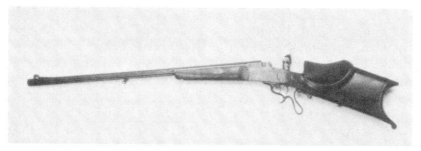

Plate Number 81

Plate Number 81 is of a larger Scheutzen rifle, weighing 11½ lbs., with a 30 5/8″ barrel and an overall length of 47″. The caliber is 8.15 x 46R with a bore diameter of .308 and a groove diameter of .319. The band of this rifle is engraved "V. KERN NURNBERG," with German proof marks.

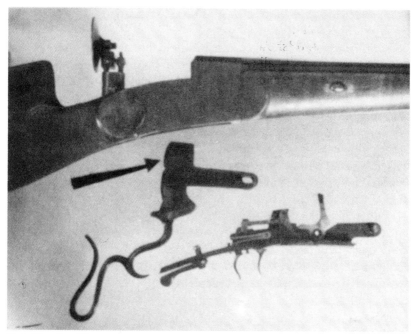

Plate Number 82

Plate Number 82 pictures the action parts and lower tang separated from the receiver. The arrow on the photo indicates the only place where the rear of the block engages the frame. This portion of the block is beveled back slightly to keep it from opening under pressure. The hinge pin does not take any of the strain of firing the piece. I have knowledge of other fascinating German and Austrian single shot rifles, but again, have not been able to obtain good photographs and details.

81

A Swiss Martini somewhat similar to the one illustrated on Page 319, Figure C in *Volume One Single Shot Rifles* with an odd chamber, has come to light lately. This rifle is in caliber 7.5 Schmidt-Rubin. Rimless cartridges are rather uncommon in this type rifle, but this caliber is not unexpected since the piece was made in Switzerland.

The problem is an oversized neck and large freebore ahead of the case. The groove diameter of the barrel is .302, but there is a long area between the neck and the bore which varies in diameter from .334 to .328. This may have been intended to accommodate a paper patched bullet, hand seated in front of the cartridge. However, it would seem .328 is way too large for such a bullet. The transition between the throat and rifling is extremely gradual and smooth. If a paper patch bullet large enough to fill the throat is used, the patch would probably strip off. A normal sized patched bullet would flop around in the throat. My guess is that it was not intended for paper patch bullets but is merely a 'free-bored' throating. As to why, or what was used in it is another guess.

Plate Number 83 shows a German single shot action which fits into the pattern generally alluded to by me in *Volume Three Boys' Rifles* as the Schmidt-Habermann basic action. These actions were sold to, and used by, various custom barrel makers and gunsmiths for their own custom productions. This illustration depicts the right side of the opened action. Caliber of the rifle is 8.15 x 46R. This is a strong falling block action with a rather massive lever, not part of the trigger guard. Frame was case hardened. Triggers are an excellent double set design. Action is scroll engraved. Trigger group detachable. The blued barrel is marked "BOHLER-ANTINITSTAHL ED. GROTHE-SOHNSTENDAL." This is a sporting rifle with a Bavarian sporting pattern stock. Has German silver bead front sight on a ramp integral with barrel. Upper flat of octagon barrel milled to accept a sliding rear barrel sight, which is missing. No provision for tang rear sight.

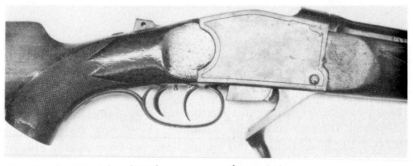

Plate Number 83   Schmidt-Habermann—another variation.

(Photo: J. Miles Griggs).

Plate Number 84 shows another rifle with the same action. (Essentially the same, that is). This rifle is also in the 8.15 x 46R caliber, also with no serial number. Finish, like *Plate Number 83*, was also casehardened, though little remains today in the way of hardening colors. This rifle has the same seat on rear of barrel for the sliding rear barrel sight, and also a base on the tang for a removeable tang sight. This base is made integral with the upper tang.

The barrel is marked ROGHLING, LOUTS, HELLFRITSCH, BERLIN. ELEKTRA STAHL." Two views of this action are shown; a side view, and one of the lower part with the action opened. The present owner says he has always attributed the manufacture of these actions to TELL. However, I am of the opinion they fit into my Schmidt-Haberman classification quite neatly. How about you?

I have seen other actions of this general appearance, varying in minor details from the ones illustrated, which I am sure are of this S-H family. The variations could be explained by different years of issue, improved models, etc?

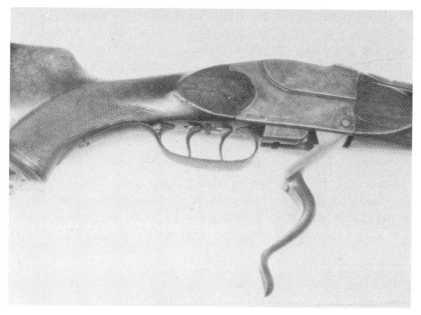

Plate Number 84   Schmidt-Habermann. (Photo: J. Miles Griggs).

Now, two deluxe American Single Shot Rifles which will take your eyes I am sure.

C. B. Holden

Plate Number 85 shows a C. B. Holden offhand pattern rifle. We showed some pieces by this maker in *Volume Two—More Single Shot Rifles.*

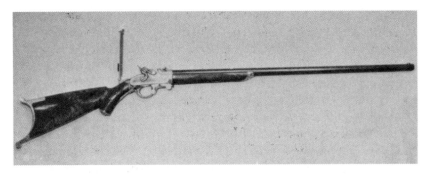

Plate Number 85   C. B. Holden Offhand Rifle. (Photo: Ron Peterson).

Barrel and receiver are both marked 19, which would be the serial number. This number also appears on all action parts and screws, as well as on the long range vernier rear sight. Rear sight staff is 6" long. Barrel is full round, 32" long, about #3 weight, blued and caliber appears to be .40-70 Sharps Straight, or very similar. A .40-70 SS case will not entirely enter the chamber (at present I do not have a chamber cast of this one). Action frame, forend tip and butt plate are engraved and nickel-plated. Lock and false side plate on other side of action are engraved and casehardened. Frame is brass or bronze. Wood is fancy grained American walnut. The manual extractor, Holden pattern on top of frame, is blued. Checkered grip and forend. Barrel is rifled with *12* lands and grooves. Weight 10 lbs., 52" long overall.

Farrow

The second rifle is a two-barreled Farrow outfit. This is depicted on *Plate Number 86.* This rifle is completely unmarked but is unmistakably a Farrow. One barrel is 30 inches long, full octagon, 7/8" across flats in .22 centerfire, (.22 WCF). It has 14 lands and

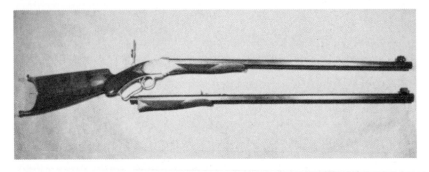

Plate Number 86   Farrow with two barrels. (Photo: Ron Peterson).

grooves and is about No. 2 in weight. No rear sight slot. The second barrel is 34", full octagon 1" across and a rear barrel sight. Both are blued. The sights are Winchester hooded Wind Gauge front, and a vernier rear is mounted on the tang at receiver. This action is made of steel or iron and is nickel-plated as is the Farrow pattern Swiss butt plate. The wood used is French walnut. It has a right hand use cheekpiece and checkered at grip and both forends. Weight with smaller barrel is 8 lbs. Overall length 48". The extra long barrel and forend weigh 6¾ lbs. This rifle has a tapered takedown pin which drives out from right to left.

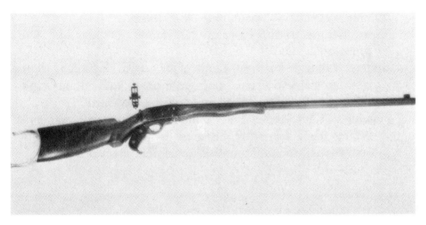

Plate Number 87   (From the David Cox Collection.)

Plate Number 87 illustrates the Standard grade Farrow Target Rifle, which is described as follows:

Name of Rifle: Farrow.

Model: Standard Grade Target.

Maker: Milton Farrow.

Markings: None.

Action Type: Lever operated dropping breechblock with reverse double set triggers. The action has a transverse barrel holding pin.

Caliber: .32-40.

Barrel length: 30" full octagon barrel. .938" at muzzle and has 14 lands and grooves with gain twist rifling.

Sights: Standard Grade Farrow vernier tang sight adjustable for windage and elevation. Non-adjustable hooded front.

Remarks: This rifle has the standard non-checkered wood with a nickel-plated brass butt plate. The trigger guard loop has rosewood panels, (possibly added after rifle left the factory?)

Plate Number 88 shows another two barrel Farrow outfit. This is a deluxe grade described as follows:

Name of rifle: Farrow Target Rifle.

Model: Deluxe grade.

Maker: Milton Farrow.

Markings: On top flat of barrel, Farrow Arms Co. Brass butt plate has "117" stamped inside and .38-55 barrel has "66" stamped on bottom flat.

Serial Number: ?

Action type: Lever operated dropping block with reverse double set triggers. Action has transverse pin to interchange barrels.

Caliber: One .32-40 barrel, one .38-55 barrel.

Barrel Length: Both barrels are half round, 30" long and .806" at muzzle.

Sights: Deluxe Farrow tang sight with cylinder sleeve micrometer elevations and calibrated half moon type windage adjustment. Non-windage hooded front.

Remarks: Each barrel has 12 lands and grooves, gain twist rifling; each forend is threaded to accommodate a palm rest. Pistol grip and forends bear skipline checkering.

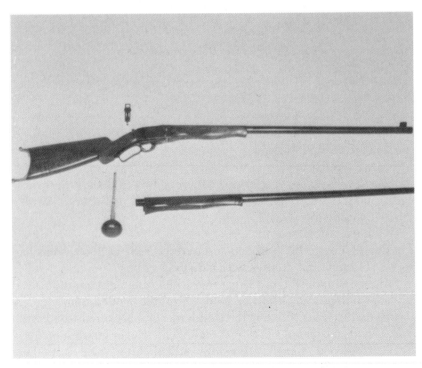

Plate Number 88   Farrow Deluxe Two Barrel Rifle. (Photo: David Cox Collection).

Plate Number 89 shows both rifles together, the Standard and Deluxe Grades for comparison.

Plate Number 90 illustrates close-ups of the actions and tang rear sight of both rifles.

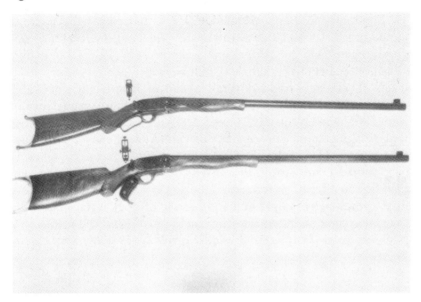

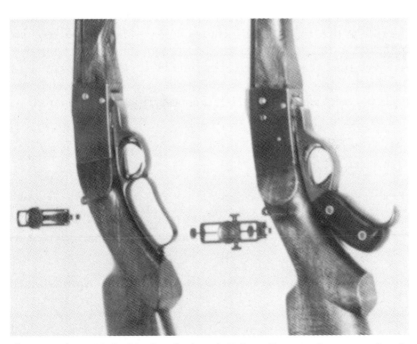

Plate Numbers 89 & 90 Standard and Deluxe Farrows shown together for comparison. Lower photo shows breech sections and rear sights.

(Photos: David Cox Collection).

Phoenix

A rifle which is unmistakably a Phoenix single shot made on a nickel-finished brass frame is next. This frame has no name or serial number on it anywhere. The barrel (possibly a replacement) is an "E. Remington & Sons" 31½" long. This barrel has the name as quoted, and on under side of the barrel, ahead of the forearm wood are stamped "44S $\substack{00 \\ 0}$ (three small circles) VW PG." Has a non-adjustable rear barrel sight, and a globe front sight very much like a Beach. There is a small dovetail ahead of front sight slot which suggests a dovetailed scale for a Remington Wind Gauge hooded front. This barrel possibly started life on a Remington R.B. Long Range rifle as some are seen in this caliber with such 2-dovetailed front sights. The buttstock of this interesting Phoenix is of fancy wood with no checkering. Brass Swiss butt plate, nickel-plated. The stock-holding screw enters from the lower tang. This stock has a slight "perch belly" lower line and bottom of stock is flat. There is a decorative panel inletted into the stock, just behind the frame. The trigger is plain but hammer and breech block have very coarse checkering. An odd one.

J. D. Wilkinson

In *More Single Shot Rifles* pages 162 and 163, I mentioned a specimen of the J. D. Wilkinson Rifle. No illustration was shown of the rifle at that time, but is included here on *Plate Numbers 91 and 92.* First a full length photo and second showing the forestock removed from the rifle. Barrel length is 28½", tapered octagonal. It has blade front sight and a tip-up rear sight. The receiver was probably color casehardened but those colors have now departed.

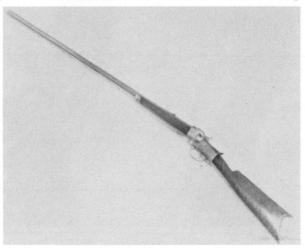

Plate Number 91   J. D. Wilkinson Rifle. (Photo: Leo Cook).

88

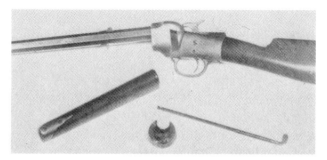

Plate Number 92   J.D. Wilkinson Rifle disassembled. (Photo: Leo Cook)

On Plate Numbers 93 and 94 is an interesting sight. This is a single shot rifle I have not encountered before. It is a sporting or, possibly, target piece and has no markings of any kind. No names, numbers, etc. are to be found on any part, so it is unknown to me and to its present owner. This rifle has a 26" octagon barrel, caliber .40-70 B.N. (Sharps or Remington). Has a blade front sight and an open rear barrel sight. No checkering on grip or forestock. The smooth operating action cocks upon the opening stroke of the under lever. The action frame is casehardened. This piece is shown in the hopes some collector or reader may be able to identify it. We realize this may be another one-of-a-kind, and it is very hard to pin down and identify pieces which have no markings whatsoever upon them.

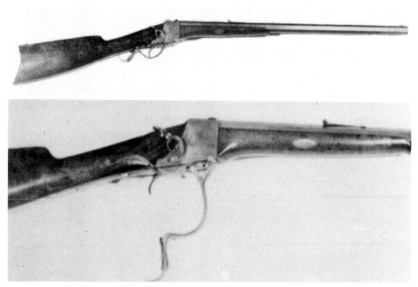

Plate Numbers 93 & 94   An unknown single shot rifle in .40-.70 B.N. (Photos: Leo Cook)

M. A. Moses

Another little known maker of single shot rifles in New York was Myron Moses who used a rifle system not unlike the Maynard, but used a reloadable steel case. I am indebted again to Mr. H. J. Swinney for the following notes on Moses.

A photograph of one of the Moses' breech-loading rifles and one of the cartridges is shown in *Gun Report,* February 1965, page 21. Both the rifle and the cartridges are said to be numbered 37 on all parts, and the rifle is said to be marked "m." Moses Molene N.Y. 1857." Because of the very obvious misspelling of the place-name "Malone," I don't trust the date.

The Grand Rapids Museum has another of these rifles, whose serial number I do not know. Martin Retting's 1953 catalog included (item C-700) a Moses breech-loader with serial number 57. In the sale of the Luce collection about 1948, one of these guns was item 220, and was purchased by Milton Clow; the same gun was resold a year later in the auction of the Clow collection. The Wisconsin Historical Society in Madison has an example of the rifle; and, the Adirondack Museum in Blue Mountain Lake, New York, also has one which is serial number 68. The barrel of the Adirondack Museum example is stamped "Remington" under the breech, but the barrel of the one in Wisconsin is stamped "Allen & Thurber/Worcester Cast Steel," suggesting that Moses made enough of these so that he changed his barrel supplier from time to time. See *Plate Numbers 95 and 96.*

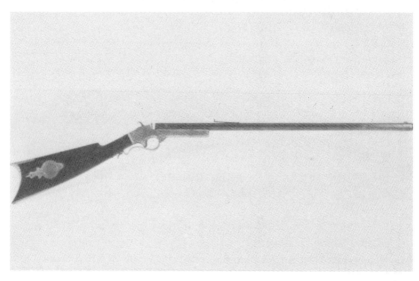

Plate Number 95   Myron Moses Rifle. (Photo: Pictorials Materials Collection, Grand Rapids Public Museum.)

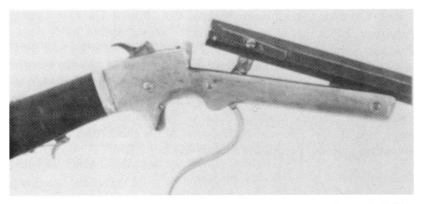

Plate Number 96 (Photo: Pictorial Materials Collection, Grand Rapids Public Museum).

So far as I have been able to discover, Moses first appears in contemporary records in Boyd's New York State Business Directory for 1859, where he is listed as a gunsmith of Malone. In the Census of the United States for 1860, he is shown as being 35 years of age, which would establish his date of birth at about 1825. He patented his breech-loader on September 30, 1862, with patent number 36571. He continued to be listed as a gunsmith in various sources through the New York State Census of 1875, in which he was shown as being 52 years of age. I have found no listing of him after that.

He advertised more or less continuously in the Malone newspapers from at least January 1, 1859 through July 2, 1874, but I have found no advertisement in his name after that. Originally, he advertised single and double-barreled rifles, as did most muzzle-loading gunsmiths of the day, but beginning in late 1862, he advertised his patent breech loader. The ad carried a cut of a pistol presumably built on this system, and of one of the cartridges. The text said in part "the most simple and durable of any rifle invented. It requires no rod to load, no patch for the ball, no starter, no loss of cartridge when discharged, can be reloaded and returned to the barrel and used any number of times."

The Directory of Franklin and Clinton Counties for 1862-63 (published in Ogdensburg, New York in 1862) carries an extensive advertisement for these guns:

Rifles' Rifles'
Myron Moses

Would respectfully invite the attention of the Public to his NEW and SUPERIOR style of Breech Loading Rifles & Pistols, which will be furnished with any number of Cartridge Cases desired on Short Notice. All kinds of gun repairs promptly attended to and Charges reasonable. Shop near his residence on Duane Street, Malone, N.Y.

Col. Gardner (*Small Arms Makers,* Col. Robert Gardner Crown Publisher, 1963) lists Moses as follows: "Moses, Myron A., Malone, Franklin County, N.Y. The census of 1860 indicates he had $600 invested in the business and employed one hand at $25 per month. During the year ending June 1, 1860, he bought gun materials at $400, made 15 rifles valued at $375 and did job work at $650. He patented a breech loading firearm September 1862 (#36,571), employing a steel reloadable chamber. Made these rifles of his own invention and also percussion muzzle-loading rifles."

W. H. Baker

W. H. Baker began as a muzzle-loading gun maker in central New York sometime in the 1840's or 1850's. Eventually he began to build three-barrel breech-loading hammer guns, and finally came to Syracuse where he established the Baker Gun Company. Very shortly, L. C. Smith took the company over, and the subsequent production was marked "L. C. Smith, maker, the Baker gun" until Smith's people came out with their own design. Baker, in the meantime established the Syracuse Gun and Forging Company, which produced a new gun of his design in the 1880's. Soon Baker was out of that company too, and removed to Ithaca, where he was instrumental in the establishment of the Ithaca Gun Company, which produced guns, again, to his design. Leaving there sometime in the '90's, he went to Batavia, New York, and established the last of the Baker Gun companies, which produced the well-known Batavia Leader, among other designs. Thus, he was responsible for a large number of the successful early breech-loading shotguns made in this country. Since he made shotguns with rifle barrels, it may be that he also made single or double rifles too. (Incidentally, Daniel Lefever made at least one or two double-barreled rifles in the famous Syracuse Shop.)

L. W. Tisdel

I have mentioned Luther W. Tisdel before, and now I wish to show you some of his products.

Plate Number 97 illustrates the first Tisdel single shot rifle and its specifications are as follows:

Name of Rifle: Tisdel.

Model: Sporting Rifle.

Maker: L. W. Tisdel.

Serial Number: "281" marked on lower tang and buttstock.

Marked: On top flat of barrel: L. W. Tisdel, Scranton, Pa. Cast Steel.

Action type: Barrel rotates to the right to load (like the Rupertus) instead of a latch, a large friction bolt parallel to bore is accessible under the forearm.

Caliber: .45-70.

Barrel length: 30" tapered octagon to .865" at muzzle.

Sights: Blade front and buckhorn rear barrel sight.

Remarks: Barrel and butt plate are browned as is also metal extension at rear of forend. Action is case hardened.

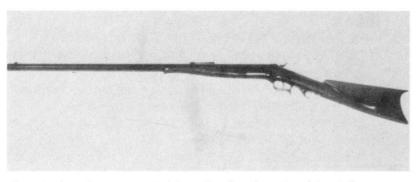

Plate Number 97   An L. W. Tisdel .45-70 Rifle. (Photo: David Cox Collection).

Plate Number 98 depicts another Tisdel sporter rifle. The data on this piece follows:

Name of rifle: Tisdel.

Model: Sporting rifle.

Maker: L. W. Tisdel.

Marked: On top flat of barrel: L. W. Tisdel, Scranton, Pa., Cast Steel.

Action type: Tisdel twist-open. Rear section tangs and trigger guard are brass. Front section cast iron or steel. Rebounding hammer.

Caliber: .32-40 (B. & M.?) Twist 1-14. .321" in grooves.

Barrel length: 32 1/8". Tapered octagon about #2 weight. Rifling 7 grooves, R.H. Twist.

Sights: Open sporting rear and blade front.

Remarks: Cheekpiece stock of fancy walnut. Forearm has ebony insert (as Winchester). "Percussion" type butt plate with separate bottom toe plate. Weight is 9¾ lbs.

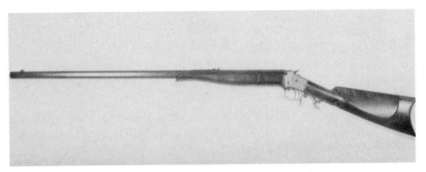

Plate Number 98   Tisdel Rifle, .32-40 caliber. (Photo: Michael Roberts).

Still another Tisdel, this one an interesting offhand rifle is shown on *Plate Number 99.* It is described as follows:

Name of rifle: Tisdel.

Model: Gallery Scheutzen.

Maker: L. W. Tisdel.

Serial Number: On lower tang '275.'

Marked: On top flat of barrel. L. W. Tisdel, Scranton, Pa. On palmrest: 'U. Surflue.'

Action type: Tisdel twist open, of cast steel, case hardened. Double set triggers, rebounding hammer.

Caliber: .22 Long Rifle R.F.

Barrel length: 28" #2 Winchester barrel.

Butt Plate: European type Swiss butt plate. Top knob is the upper holding screw.

Sights: Modern windage front and vernier tang rear, by Wm. Oates & J. Lofland.

Remarks: The owner of this rifle is of the opinion this was originally built as a centerfire rifle. If you will look closely at *Plate Number 100* you will see that the barrel is threaded into the breech piece at a very slight angle, thus causing a rimfire barrel to work on what was possibly a centerfire action. This work is very skillfully done. The present sights were installed by the current owner as the rifle came to him without sights. Luther Tisdel was a fine workman, although the design of the action has some flaws. The owner reports the actions are smooth and a pleasure to use. He is loathe to fire the .32-40 rifle even with black powder loads.

Luther W. Tisdel is listed as a gun maker in the Scranton, Pennsylvania City Directories as early as 1866, on Pennsylvania Street near Lackawanna.

1875 The shop was at 112 Franklin Avenue.

1883 "L. W. Tisdell (Sic) Manufacturer and dealer in guns,

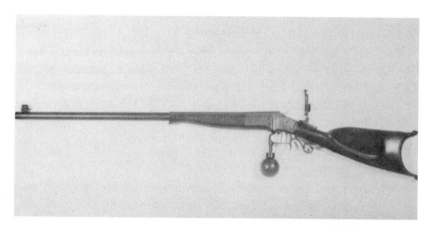

Plate Numbers 99 & 100 Another L. W. Tisdel rifle, in .22 Long Rifle rimfire—possibly converted from centerfire. See Plate 100 for close-up of breech section. (Photos: Michael Roberts).

pistols and ammunition, 120 Franklin, Scranton. Repairing of all kinds promptly done."

1885 Shop at 120 Franklin Street. His home was now at 925 Slocum.

1905 At 96 S. Washington Ave.

Gardner (*Small Arms Makers*, by Colonel Robert Gardner, Crown Publisher 1963) states:

"Tisdale (Sic) Luther W., Scranton, Lackawanna County, Pa., 1848-51 and probably later. The census of 1870 states he was located in Germantown, Luzerne County, had $1,000.00 invested in the business and employed no help. During the year ending June 1876, he purchased materials in the amount of $350.00 and produced guns and miscellaneous articles valued at $1040.00. A maker of heavy percussion rifles he died about 1890."

Kirkwood

Plate Number 101 shows you a rifle which is seldom seen. This is the Kirkwood. A close-up view of the breech portion of the Kirkwood is shown on *Plate Number 102*. The specifications are:

Name of rifle: David Kirkwood.

Model: Target rifle.

Maker: Mortimer & Kirkwood, Boston, Mass.

Serial Number: None.

Markings: None.

Action type: Lever operated, dropping-block cocking indicator on right side of receiver. The knurled lever on side of action manually cams back cocking indicator to act as safety.

Caliber: .40-70 B.N.

Barrel length: 30", 1" across flats.

Sights: Rifle fitted with 32" Malcolm telescopic sight. No provision for iron sights of any kind.

Remarks: Action, barrel and butt plate are blued. Delicate scroll engraving on frame, tang and butt plate. Dark, burl walnut bears fine checkering, with horn pistol grip cap and forend tip.

The David Kirkwood, or Mortimer & Kirkwood is a well made rifle. Kirkwood apprenticed in Scotland and England before setting up shop in Boston. Gardner gives the following notes on Kirkwood:

"Kirkwood, David, Mortimer & Kirkwood, gunmakers of Boston were active 1875-80 Partnership of Henry Mortimer & David Kirkwood. Kirkwood operated alone at 23 Elm Street, 1882-88. His sons continued thereafter as Kirkwood Bros. David Kirkwood was granted the following patents: With Henry Mortimer, Lock for firearms, November 9, 1875 (#169,710). Breech loading firearms June 12, 1877 (#191,862). Breech loading firearms, October 12, 1880 (#233,256) October 26, 1880 (#233,773), April 12, 1881 (#240,147), November 27, 1883 (#289,273) May 19, 1885 (#318,001)," and following data on Henry Mortimer:

"Mortimer, Henry, Partners with David Kirkwood in Mortimer & Kirkwood, Boston, Mass. With David Kirkwood granted a patent on a lock for firearms, November 9, 1875 (#169,710)."

Plate Number 101   The Kirkwood Rifle. (Photo: David Cox Collection).

96

Plate Number 102 Breech section of Kirkwood. Rifle. (Photo: David Cox Collection).

The Warner-Greene Rifle

The Warner-Greene is somewhat of an enigma. This company contracted to make 4,000 Civil War Carbines; but, specimen shown on *Plate Number 103* is certainly a sporting rifle, not a military carbine, while the serial number falls in the range attributed to the Civil War Carbine production. This has a barrel 4″ longer than the carbines and it is obviously a factory original sporting model.

There are no flaws in the cast brass receiver and there is no explanation why they would pull a number in the middle of the military contract for purposes of making a sporting rifle. Perhaps an official of the company or some bureaucrat in the government wanted to go hunting?

The specifications of this Warner-Greene follow:

Name of Rifle: Warner-Greene.

Model: Sporting.

Maker: Greene Rifle Works.

Serial Number: 2983 on receiver, bottom of barrel, forend and buttstock.

Marked: On left side of receiver: "Greene Rifle Works, Worcester, Mass. Pat'd. 1864.

Action type: Breech block is hinged on right and rolls over like the Phoenix, sliding release latch located on left side of receiver.

Caliber: .56-50 Spencer rimfire.

Barrel length: 28″ round. Weight 8 lbs.

Remarks: Receiver and butt plate are non-plated brass. The wood is deluxe burled walnut.

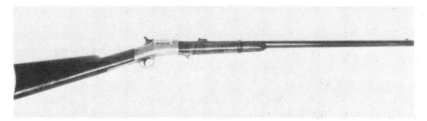

Plate Number 103   The Warner-Greene Sporting Rifle.

(Photo: David Cox Collection).

C. N. Cutter

One more unusual single shot rifle which has some connections with others which are far more famous. *Plate number 104* illustrates a specimen of the C. N. Cutter rifle.

    Name of rifle: Cutter.

    Model: Target Rifle??

    Maker: C. N. Cutter.

    Serial Number: None.

    Marked: On top flat of barrel. "C.N. Cutter, Worcester, Mass." No other markings.

    Action type: Lever around front of trigger guard rotates to right to release tip-up barrel.

    Caliber: .38 Long centerfire.

    Barrel length: 26½" Part round.

    Sights: Blade front and notch rear barrel sight. The tang rear sight is like those commonly seen on Wesson tip-up sporting rifles.

    Remarks: The frame, release lever and checkered steel butt plate are nickel-plated. C. N. Cutter was a Frank Wesson employee and U.S. Patent office records indicate their collaboration on patent applications.

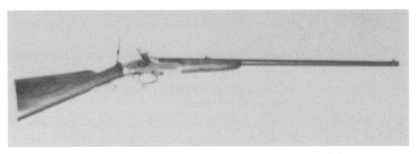

Plate Number 104   A C. N. Cutter .38 Long Centerfire rifle. (Photo: David Cox Collection).

The H. W. Z. Action

Finally, a brief mention of a German action which is seldom seen, the H. W. Z.

The action was introduced in about 1912 in Germany and persisted, in a somewhat limited way, thru several variations, until about 1930. As far as is known at present time, it was made only in .22 rimfire caliber.

Viewed from the side this action appears to be similar to the Martini system, however the side walls of the frame immediately to the rear of the barrel housing portion are rather deeply and sharply cut down in a circular pattern. This is no doubt to facilitate loading the small rimfire .22 cartridge into the breech of the barrel. The finger lever opening for the triggers is somewhat longer than is usual, and the front trigger on at least one specimen is adjustable for reach, i.e. it seems to be capable of being moved backward or forward on a slotted track. The reason for this is unknown.

The action displays an interesting pivoted firing pin on a hammer driven by a coil spring compressed between this hammer and the lever. This particular specimen has had some remodeling performed upon it, as it has been restocked, apparently by an amateur, and it has also been rebarreled. Perhaps we'll turn up more details on this system later.

As mentioned above, it appears to be similar to a Martini, however it is not such a system, as it has no rear pivoted tipping block, but is a falling block pattern action.

V

F. Wesson—Maker

The products of Franklin Wesson, touched on briefly in Volume One and continued through Volume Two and Volume Three, continue to be of great interest. I know they are a source of much interest to many others, as well they might be. The amazing variety of his rifles is a source of continuing surprise.

On page 57 in *Volume Two More Single Shot Rifles*, I talked about some unusual markings on a tip-up Wesson rifle. This was a .44 caliber Wesson and I suggest you re-read the part concerning that rifle, for now I have more information which will throw some light (I hope) on the puzzle. Dr. John Crawford had a Wesson carbine and he reported his barrel was stamped on top "J. CUTLER FULLER, SHANGHAE, Pat. Oct. 26, 1859, Nov. 11, 1862." In addition to this, it is marked along the right side of the barrel near the frame with eight Japanese characters. These have been interpreted as meaning "Nine Year Seven Tong King Fou." This, in our marking, would be—(according to the interpretation)—the "Ninth Year of the Reign of Emperor Meiji, Number 747, City of Tokyo." This would place it about the year 1876, Tokyo, Japan. In the Japanese time-keeping system, the year 1968, (which is the year Dr. Crawford wrote me about the translation), would be 1943. Showa is the present Emperor. Before him, was Emperor Taisho and preceding him was Emperor Meiji. This would place the time correctly, as the gun was manufactured sometime after 1862; 1967 was the 100th Anniversary of Emperor Meiji, therefore, deducting 100 years from 1967 leaves the year 1867; the ninth year of his rule would have been 1876. Further, it is believed the Wesson rifle was imported by J. Cutler Fuller of Shanghae and was made for him by Frank Wesson. Many guns of that time were custom made for other importers with their special markings. This spelling of "Shanghae" is the old one, it being changed to "Shanghai" sometime later.

This rifle has a brass receiver, forearm piece, triggerguard, and buttplate, with steel barrel, hammer and trigger. It also has sling swivels on the barrel and on the stock, and is serial number 8262.

Thank you, Dr. Crawford, for throwing this light on a long mystifying rifle marking.

I would like to mention two or three other tip-up Wesson specimens. One of these is a rifle in .44 caliber centerfire. This is marked on top of the barrel in the usual place, "Frank Wesson, Worcester, Mass. Pat'd. Oct. 25, 1859;" most of the 1862 patent date is unreadable. It has the two-leaved barrel sight, both leaves rigidly connected in an "L" shape. This rifle is missing the slotted barrel link, but has no sign of an extractor and, apparently, never had one. No cuts in barrel, no way of extracting a spent shell except by means of a rod.

Another Wesson, also in .44 caliber, has Frank Wesson, Worcester, Mass. markings, and the patent date of 1859; but, does not have any mention of the 1862 patent. It also has the marking "B. Kitteredge & Co., Cincinnati, Ohio," as has been observed before. This also has the tip-up rear barrel sight marked for 250 and 500 yards. The barrel restraining flat member outside is marked "Pat. Pending."

Another tip-up Wesson, this one a later version is marked with the 1859 and 1862 patents, and also, the hammer is stamped on the left side "Pat'd. Apr. 9, 1872." The serial number 318 is on the triggerguard. The frame is the flat sided frame often observed. The barrel is a 25½" pattern, 7½" octagon, 18¼" round and is chambered for an odd cartridge. Bore slugs .310; a .25-20 SS shell chambers well and when shot and expanded, mikes under the rim to .318. The mouth diameter outside is .318. This is another Frank Wesson odd-ball caliber. The closest thing to it seems to be the .32-30 Remington.

Another tip-up rifle, apparently a .38 caliber of some sort, has a 25½" octagonal barrel; .847 at breech and .721 at muzzle. Twist is 1 turn in 25½" and has 5 lands and grooves. This barrel has both the 1859 and 1862 patent dates; also, the 1872 patent date on the left side of the hammer. The breech is fitted with two firing pins, both spring loaded for retraction. One a rimfire pin, the other centerfire, and the hammer has the adjustable block to change from one to the other. The frame is of iron, flat sides, nickel-plated. This has the usual iron, plain post front sight and the adjustable for elevation rear barrel sight. The serial number is 167, stamped on trigger guard, underside of barrel at breech, at forward inside end of receiver and stamped into stock and butt plate. This chamber is as follows: Rim clearance .465, rim thickness .057, diameter at casehead .388, diameter at case mouth .383, bore is .375 groove diameter and land to land is .369. This chamber will accept a fired .38 Long Colt readily, .38 Special case slightly long and case rim of .38 Special needs slight urging to chamber. .38 Short and Long rimfires will readily chamber. The above measurements taken from a metal chamber cast. Apparently a Wesson for the Wesson long centerfire or rimfire cartridges.

The next Wesson rifle is different. *Plate Number 105* shows a Wesson Number One Mid-Range and Sporting Rifle. A specimen of this rifle from my own collection was shown in *Volume Two More Single Shot Rifles*, and this one appears to be almost identical. Serial number of this rifle is 2. The frame and lever are nickled brass. The frame is numbered just behind the lever pivot screw. All internal parts are number stamped 2, including the breech block, trigger, hammer, all screws and small parts. The breech block is color case hardened. The 28" part octagon, part round barrel is numbered 2 beneath the forearm. The only other markings on the barrel are "F. WESSON MAKER, WORCESTER, MASS." on the top flat just ahead of the rear sight.

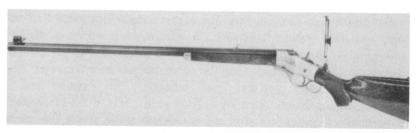

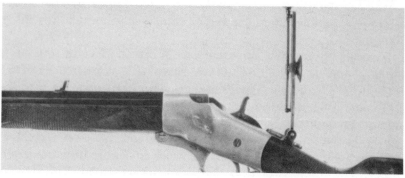

Plate Number 105   F. Wesson Mid-Range & Sporting Rifle. (Lower) Close-up of action and tang sight. (Photos: Edward Haight).

102

Taken from the chamber cast of this barrel are the following dimensions:

Length: 2 5/16"
Neck Diameter: 0.425"
Diameter under rim: 0.462"
Groove diameter: 0.411", 5 grooves.

The owner reports he has made some cases for the rifle from 9.3 x 74R brass. The buttstock and forearm are made of fancy walnut with the usual very high gloss varnish finish common to this model. There is a checkered steel shotgun type butt plate also numbered 2. The front sight is missing. The open rear barrel/sight is a typical non-adjustable Wesson sight. The tang sight is the long range vernier type and is numbered 2 on both the staff and base. The disc in this sight is not original but is from a Lyman sight. The buttstock has a heel sight base also numbered 2 on the base and on two screw heads. Here is another fine example of the scarcest of all American rifles, and these certainly rank in that specially rarified category occupied by very few rifles and pistols in the world.

On *Plate Number 106* is another Franklin Wesson rifle. This is a specimen of the Number 2 falling block rifle, usually referred to as the Long- and Mid-Range Model. This is because you will find them chambered for Mid-Range cartridges, and at other times they are made for cartridges generally used at longer ranges.

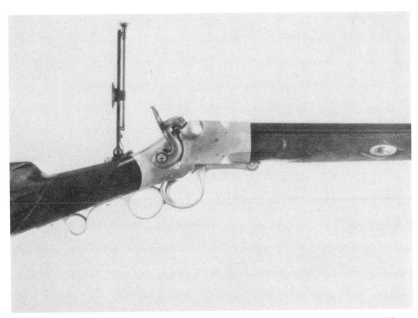

Plate Number 106   F. Wesson Long & Mid-Range Rifle, .42 Wesson B.N. caliber. (Photo: Edward Haight).

This specimen is chambered for the same cartridge as one described in *Volume Two More Single Shot Rifles*. It takes the .42 Wesson bottle necked case, which is the same as the .42 Russian Berdan cartridge. To refresh your memory on that, here are the dimensions of this chamber compared with the .42 Russian Berdan cartridge:

Chamber Dimensions:	Chamber Cast	42 Russian
Rim Dia.	0.625"	0.639"
Head Dia.	0.520"	0.516"
Shoulder Dia.	0.509"	0.511"
Neck Dia.	0.448"	0.448"
Bullet Dia.	—	0.433"
Case Length	—	2.24"

VI

The Ballard Rifle

Information on the Ballard continues to crop up. New information which comes in is mainly on certain variations from the normal pattern of rifles, as there are no new factory models to discover. Nevertheless, rifles with certain quirks do pop up now and then, and this makes the Ballard continue to be a fascinating rifle.

I discussed the pre-Marlin Ballards from time to time before and now wish to mention a few more. A Ball and Williams Ballard rifle, serial number 36 in .38 rimfire caliber has the automatic extractor described on page one, *More Single Shot Rifles.* This early serial number certainly is worthy of mention; also, this rifle has a part octagon barrel. The octagon portion is 7¼″ long and the round part tapers from 1 15/16″ at rear to 13/16″ at the muzzle.

The rifle is marked:

"Merrimack Arms & Mfg. Co."
Newburyport Mass.
Ballards Patent
Nov. 3, 1861"

Serial number 20224 is on the top of receiver and on top of barrel at breech. There is also the number "50" on top of the barrel, this indicated .50 caliber. The hammer is marked "Patented Jan. 5, 1864."

This appears to be a standard three band military model, with patent hammer, for cartridge or percussion ignition. The extractor is on bottom of forehand, which is standard for this early Ballard.

There are three screws to hold butt plate, one on top and two in curve of butt. The reason for the third screw is unknown. Has standard swivels on middle barrel band and rear of buttstock.

So far we have a standard early Ballard, but here is an odd part. This gun is equipped with what looks to be an original ramrod. Rod is 29 15/16" long swell-head type, similar to, but not the same as, an 1864 Springfield. Ramrod is mounted on right hand side of gun in approximately a 3 o'clock position at rear and 4 o'clock position on barrel end. It is attached at breech by a stud into side of the receiver into which the end of the rod is threaded. Attachment on barrel end is a metal holder screw fastened to the wood with four screws, and is 10/16" long mounted five inches from end of barrel. Most important, this all looks original and not a later addition to the gun. I have had no other mention of ramrods for early Ballards.

A 1913 issue of *Hunter-Trader-Trapper Magazine* contains an interesting letter and I quote from it: "I see by the February number of H-T-T 'Old Gunsmith' asks how to blue barrels. In 1872, I was running a rifling machine for the Brown Mfg. Co. They made the Ballard Rifle and the Southerner pistol. The Ballard was afterwards taken over by the Marlin Company.

"Pistol barrels were blued in hot sand. After polishing rifle barrels, a pine plug was driven tightly in each end, projecting about 5 inches. All handling was by these plugs, then rolled in air-slaked lime to remove all trace of oil, wiped with a clean rag and brushed over with diluted nitric acid and placed in racks for about 12 hours, then put in tank of water and boiled for 15 or 20 minutes. On taking out they were covered with a fine red rust. This was scrubbed off with a wire brush and a piece of old cord clothing. They then showed a pale blue. This process was repeated on an average of 3-4 times when the deep blue was obtained. After last wire brushing if blue was deep enough the barrel was rubbed with woolen rag and oil and beeswax. The barrel must never be touched by the fingers after being limed, till the oil and beeswax polish is on, all handling done by projecting plugs. After 2 years in the gunshop I went into a job shop but for several years I did gun repairing and have used this process with good results if I was careful, but couldn't hurry it, and comes out good."

On an early Marlin Ballard Hunters Rifle, serial number 82 appears on top of action, top of barrel, the extractor, the butt and ·forend wood, on the steel butt plate and the steel forend tip. This is a .44 caliber rifle with a reversible firing pin, and flat faced hammer with long spur. The left side of frame is marked: "J. M. Marlin Pat. Feb. 9, 1875" and the original Ballard date of "Nov. 5, 1861." The extractor is of the push-spring type in its own housing or in other words the manual, underbarrel type. This rifle has the buttstock holding screw coming out to the surface of the butt plate where it may be removed without taking off the butt plate first. This rifle has no metal damage by rust, etc., and was never blued or browned at all. Under the forearm the metal is in the white. It is apparently an interesting early transition Hunters Model.

Another early rifle reported is a Number One Marlin Hunters model with the very early number of '15.' This rifle has the round top receiver and round barrel in .44 rim- or centerfire caliber. In all other respects it is similar to those I have illustrated in the past, with one exception. The original butt plate on this piece is of the carbine type instead of the usual rifle or crescent style. It appears to be more of a military or semi-military pattern. The frame of this rifle also has the small hole on bottom rear of the frame and a corresponding hole in the lever. The pin was missing, but possibly was never installed at the factory.

I wish to show you a pair of consecutively serial numbered, engraved Ballards.

Plate Number 107 shows serial number 20341 of the pair of Brown Mfg. Co. Ballards. Serial number is on top of barrel and top flat of receiver. Forearm numbered in front of the extractor spring slot, and numbered on left rear flat of block. Number '1' marked on left flat of lever. Butt plate screws marked '41,' butt plate '41,' as well as buttstock. The buttstock bolt fits through a hole in the butt plate. Barrel length is 24", pull is 13½", combination percussion and rimfire with the rimfire pin in block. Barrel is rifled with 5 wide grooves. Bore diameter is .0410.

Plate Number 108 illustrates the companion rifle with serial number of 20342. This rifle is engraved with great similiarity to the previous one. This piece is numbered in the same areas, with the same stamp as rifle number 20341. The remaining finish of this latter rifle is not quite as good as the former. Note how the checkering of both fore— and buttstock are checkered right up to the metal on both specimens. The present owner of these rifles, Mr. Harry Egdorf of Nebraska, found one in Pennsylvania and the other in Texas.

He states "The last Merrimack serial number I am aware of is #20326, but there is an engraved Brown in Wilson's Book of *Nimschke Engraving*. It is an engraved Brown Ballard with interchangeable barrels numbered 20324. So there is some overlap on figures. All of the engraved Browns I have seen or heard of are within 17 serial numbers of each other. They may have sent a few of the first production to Nimschke for engraving to use as show pieces."

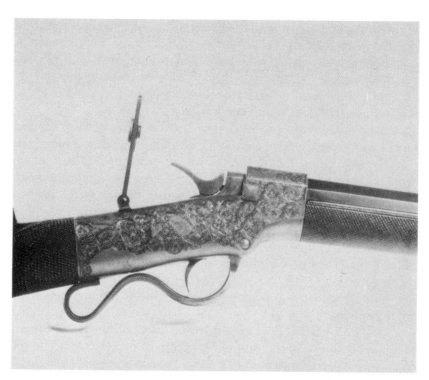

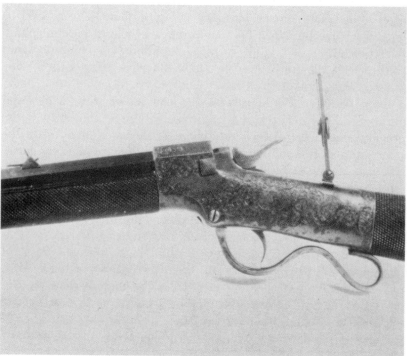

Plate Numbers 107 & 108 Engraved Brown Ballards, .38 and .44 calibers, consecutively serial numbered 20341 and 20342. (Photos: Harry W. Egdorf).

A J. M. Marlin Hunters Rifle Model 1 that was reported to me recently, bears the serial number of 278. It is numbered both on top of receiver and barrel as usual. The rifle is marked as is the one shown on plate no. 2 in *More Single Shot Rifles*. Has the automatic inside extractor, of course, and is also in .44 caliber. The rear sight is different from any seen before. It is made as follows: Tipping the sight forward brings a 'V' shaped sight up which is a box with a sliding 'V' inside a frame. This sliding box is raised or lowered by the fingers. Frame and lever both have the holes for the securing pin to join these two pieces but this pin is also missing.

Since *Boys' Rifles* was published I have had reports of three or four more Ballard Model 4 1/4 rifles authenticated. All of these rifles so far have been the same caliber as the specimen I owned and was shown in *Volume Two More Single Shot Rifles*. They are chambered for the 3 1/16″ Ideal Ballard Everlasting case. The Schoverling, Daly and Gales circular quoted in *Boys' Rifles*, page 480, lists several other cartridges which were available about this time for this Model 4 1/4 as well as possibly other models. It seems rather odd that I have not learned of such a model as the 4 1/4 made for anything other than this .40-90 Ideal case. But, possibly even before this manuscript is printed into book form, one will turn up. There are bound to be some specimens around which have not yet been reported.

I have reports, chamber casts, etc. from a very few rifles which are purported to be chambered for the legendary .40-60 Ballard cartridge. See the same chapter on Ballard mentioned previously about this one. It is possible Marlin had a cartridge early in their manufacture of the Ballard which was called a .40-60. There is no doubt the Schoverling, Daly and Gales circular illustrates one, and names one, even though it appears unlikely the actual cartridge was like the out-of-proportion case shown in the circular.

If Ballard had a .40-60 chambering and used it, it was early; (the two or three rifles reported have serial numbers before 2,000), and was no doubt discontinued early in the history of the Ballard. Some other chambers reported are so very close to the .40-60-'82 Maynard case that they may accept this one. The .40-60 Maynard is quite scarce. I never owned a rifle made by Maynard for this cartridge but did have a quantity of everlasting model 1882 cases which were .40-60 Maynard. I have not yet been able to reconcile the differences in some of these reported Ballard chambers. There is too much variance in most of them to attribute them to our sought-after .40-60 Ballard. (See Chart accompanying this chapter.)

I have seen a Ballard with original barrel which is chambered for the Remington .32-30-150 caliber cartridge. This is a Marlin Firearms model serial numbered 19694 which is late enough to warrant using that particular cartridge.

RIFLE	RIM	UNDER RIM	MOUTH	CASE LENGTH	GROOVE DIAMETER	REMARKS
Ballard, Ser. No. 1061, from Texas	.572"	.4575"	.451"	2.065"—2 1/16" under head.	.408"	Bore diameter is .400-406". This rifle takes an Everlasting-type case. Rifle shot well with blown out .30-40 cases.
Ballard No. 4½ A-I Mid-Range from Kansas.		.4595"	.456"	2 1/16" under head. Probably 2 1/8" overall.	.411-.412"	This rifle takes an Everlasting-type case. The chamber has a very slight chamfer at front end, ahead of case. Will accept .40-60 Marlin and .40-65 WCF loaded cartridges, but neither is correct.
Unknown case furnished by author and fired in above chamber three times. (1)		.453-.455"	.456"	2 1/16" under head.		This previously unknown case had been with me for years. It was shot three times in the rifle above with 18 gr. of 4227 and a .408" 300 grain bullet. Case has shallow counterbore approx. 3/16" deep.
Ballard No. 4½ A-I Mid-Range	.5045"	.461"	.455"	2 1/6" under head. 2 1/8" overall.		The difference between neck diameter and groove diameter is .046", indicating a true Everlasting case.
Ballard No. 4 Perfection Rifle—Serial No. 5712		.506-.507"	.425-.427"	2 1/6" under head. 2 1/8" overall.	.4095-.412"	This rifle is not likely chambered for our .40-60 cartridge. Given here to compare only with above.

(1) This cartridge case, fired in the chamber of the Mid-Range rifle now owned by a Kansas collector, is illustrated on *Plate Number 116*. This chambering, met with very seldom in the Ballards, always with early serial numbers, was apparently used for very early production series rifles—perhaps in the first two-four years by J. M. Marlin. No doubt abandoned early—why? Was it because the .40-63 or the .40-65 superseded it? Is it possibly in the same category as the .44-75 Ballard Everlasting in this respect?

This is a Union Hill rifle with 30" part octagon barrel on a pistol grip frame with double set triggers, long loop lever and with quite a bit of color remaining in the action receiver. The barrel has a hooded front sight, Buckhorn rear barrel sight and a tang sight of the plain non-vernier variety. The extractor is numbered '38.'

A Ballard No. 4½ rifle is in the .44-75 Everlasting, a Ballard special caliber. The chamber accepts the .44-75 2½" case. The bore diameter is .446 while groove diameter measures out to .452. This is very close to the usual .45 groove diameters, but this was probably intended for paper patched bullets which would have a nominal diameter of .446-.449. The owner has fired the rifle with fair success using .452 diameter lubricated lead bullets from a Lyman mould.

Another .44-75 Ballard is also reported as being a number 4½, but I am uncertain about the exact model since I have been unable to get more details regarding the piece. I will give the specifications of the barrel and chamber as far as I can go with them. The barrel is 28" long, has 6 grooves and lands with a bore diameter of .4435 and grooves .4512 deep. Base diameter of shell .500, length of chamber to the lands is 2.525. Action has a single trigger, loop lever, and frame is the flat sided, non-stepped pattern. This is a J. M. Marlin Model with the serial number in the 1300 series.

It's surprising how few Ballards turn up barreled and chambered for more common cartridges such as the .44-40 Winchester. This caliber was offered in some models, mainly the Number Two Model, and I have one to mention now; one of the very few I have come in contact with. This rifle, serial numbered 17,574 is marked 44W and is chambered for the .44-40. It is a Number Two, as have been the few seen. It has a 30" barrel, 12 inches of which are octagon, the balance to the muzzle, round. The frame is marked "J. M. Marlin New Haven, Conn. patented February 9, 1875, Ballard patent Nov. 5, 1861." It appears like Figure E. on Page 3 *Single Shot Rifles* with the exception of the part octagon barrel on this piece.

Plate Number 109 shows some long ago shooters of the rifles we are talking about. These photos from Herb Peck, a collector of tin types and ambrotype photographs were found by him in Nashville, Tennessee, which is Herb's home.

The photo with the two determined looking characters, shows one of them grasping the barrel of a Pacific Ballard. This photo was no doubt made in a commercial photographer's studio and illustrates interesting clothing as well as two very nonchalant appearing gentlemen equipped with stogies in their faces and all set to take off into what must have been winter weather.

Plate Number 109   Ballard buffs from long ago—note Pacific Ballard.

(Photo: Herb Peck).

Plate Number 110 is a photo of a pair of tin types in a folding double gutta percha case. This is the way tin types and ambrotypes were customarily mounted. Civil War photos of soldiers with carbines, especially Ballards, are quite rare and a pair of these is quite unique.

Plate Number 110   (Photo: Herb Peck)

Herb suggests these men could have been members of a Union Cavalry unit from nearby Kentucky. At any rate here are early Ballards in the hands of contemporary "users."

One of the more scarce Ballard models certainly is the number 5½ Montana rifle. Several have been reported to me, but upon further research turn out to be merely Pacific Ballard Number 5 rifles with extra heavy barrels upon them.

One such rifle is marked Marlin Firearms Company and is number 26721, which, in my opinion, is too high a number and too late a rifle to be a true number 5½. It has a heavy barrel, 28½" in length, 1¼" across the flats at breech and the rifle weighs 14 lbs. It is reported as being .45-100 caliber, but the case length is unknown. It has the correct double set triggers, Pacific style lever and a rifle butt plate. The latter detail, the serial number, and being manufactured by Marlin Firearms instead of J. M. Marlin puts it definitely into the heavy Pacific category. You will recall, you could get any size barrel, chambered for most anything reasonable, even as late as the period of Marlin Firearms Company.

112

A Ballard which I would say is definitely the Model 5½ Montana has serial number 9869. This has a barrel 30″ in length, 1 5/16″ across the flats ahead of receiver, stamped .45-100 2 7/8″ on top flat ahead of that receiver. Has Ballard double set triggers, finger lever as #6 in *Single Shot Rifles* and butt plate as #4 in that book, sights are the same as usually seen on the model. Blade front, Ballard long rear barrel sight. This has all the correct ear marks of the Montana and very few rifles have all these features intact.

A rather unusual Number 5 Pacific rifle is number 23840, a 36″ barreled piece. Barrel is full octagon, measuring 1.265 across flats at breech and 1.090″ at muzzle. The forearm has a cast pewter tip. (These are found occasionally). Rifle is a Marlin Firearms model on a Pacific double set trigger action with steel rifle butt plate. The barrel is marked .45-100 and is chambered for the .45 (2.6″) Sharps case. Rifle weighs 14 pounds. All numbers match correctly on this one.

Plate Number 111 illustrates both sides of an unusual Ballard. This is a factory engraved version of the 3-F or Fine Gallery Rifle, Serial No. is 21939. Variations of the basic 3-F rifle are scarce and engraved versions quite rare. This rifle has a 28″ full octagon barrel for the .22 rimfire cartridge. The wood of the buttstock is fancy fiddleback walnut with a rifle or sporting type butt plate. Checkered fore and aft and forearm has a horn tip. A Marlin Firearms Company product—naturally!

Plate Number 111   A Ballard 3F Gallery Rifle, engraved. Photos show right and left side of frame. (Photos: Donald Lerner).

Plate Number 112 shows the action frame of a specially engraved Union Hill Ballard. The deer hunting scene depicted shows the buck receiving the shot from a hunter in the distance, while a doe escapes in the background. Frame is in the white which is very difficult to photograph. More details will be given on this rifle in the last chapter of this book.

Plate Number 112   A Union Hill Ballard with special engraving.

Now to securely cap this chapter on Ballards I have saved the best for last.

The rifle shown on *Plate Numbers 113 and 114* was almost forgotten and I would never have forgiven myself. This is a specimen the likes of which I have never seen nor heard of. It is a Ballard No. *4½ A-1 Special.* The Number 7-A-1 Specials that have been seen are very, very few in number; but, *this* is the only rifle filling the specifications of a No. 4½ A-1 Special, if one were ever ordered. It has a 30" Rigby pattern barrel, caliber .40-70 Ballard with a hooded Wind Gauge front sight, and someone years ago added scope blocks which are the only part not original. The action is the faceted corners, side-rebated, pistol grip pattern; engraved somewhat similar to the later #6 and #6½ actions, with game scenes instead of "Ballard A-1 Mid-Range," etc. Single checkered trigger, full loop lever. Sight on the frame is apparently original to this rifle and is the Short-Range pattern, not Mid-Range height of staff. Wood is Circassian walnut, horn shotgun-type butt plate and inlay in bottom of pistol grip face, also horn tip on forend. Finely checkered fore and aft. Has a gold plate in left side of the stock, a name and city engraved thereon. Evidently this was a presentation rifle to the man named in this plate. Serial number is in the 15,xxx range, and again, I mention it is the only rifle I ever saw or heard of with Mid-Range No. 4½ A-1 Special possibilities.

114

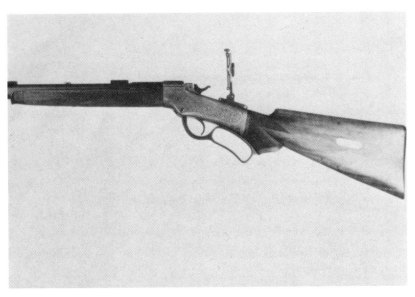

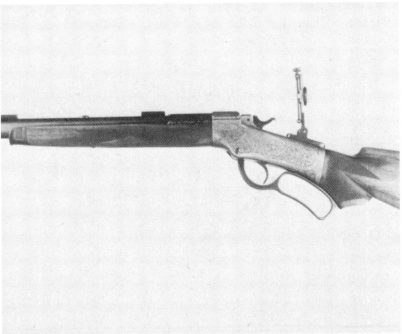

Plate Numbers 113 & 114   Ballard Model 4½ A-1 Special-Extra. This speciman is possibly the only known gun of the 4½ A-1 Special classification.

On *Plate Number 115* I show another Ballard No. 4½A-1 specimen. This is like the usual 4½A-1 I have shown before. However, the specimen, serial number 792 is chambered for the legendary .40-60 Ballard Everlasting case, 2 1/8″ long.

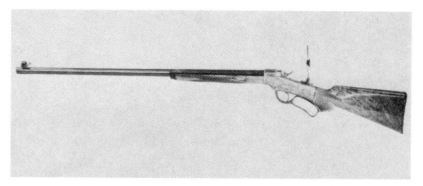

Plate Number 115   Ballard 4½ A-1 in .40-60 Ballard Everlasting.

(Photo: Edward Haight).

I list another Ballard, also a Model 4½A-1 in the explanation of
the next illustration.

Plate Number 116 illustrates the .40-60 and .44-75 Ballard
cartridges, possibly the first time they have been illustrated
anywhere. These are both *rare cartridges* and have not been
identified by any cartridge collector so far.

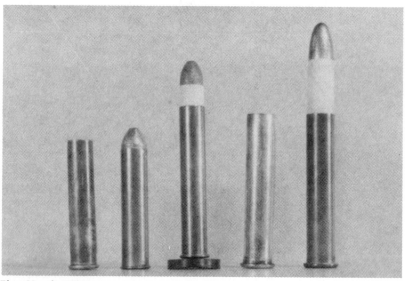

Plate Number 116

The explanation of *Plate Number 116* is as follows:

Left to right:

.40-60 Ballard Everlasting

.45-60 Wesson Straight Target (for comparison only)

.42-85 or .42-90 Wesson

.44-75 Ballard Everlasting (Nickle-plated case)

.44-75 Ballard Everlasting with Paper Patch Bullet

116

VII

Peabody and Peabody-Martini

Much coverage was given to the products of The Providence Tool Company in the last book, and there is not much to add to that. I *do* have some data on the side hammer Peabodys and will make a few notes on these.

The remarks concerning the rimfire Peabody Sporting Rifles still stand, but I wish to add the description of another. This is a Peabody Sporting Rifle, serial numbered '71' on the front of the receiver. It has a 28″ round barrel in caliber .45 *rimfire!* In appearance, this rifle is like the sporting rifle pictured in the Providence Tool Company catalogue of 1866. A detailed description of this interesting rifle follows:

> Receiver: Stamped on the front face on the center lug with the number '71' The left side of receiver is stamped "PEABODY'S PATENT, July 22, 1862" and on the right side "Man'f'd. by Providence Tool Co., Prov., R.I."

The stamping on right side is not parallel with the top and bottom line of the frame but is noticeably tilted. The frame shows some slight case colors. The center lug of the front face is drilled and tapped for the military cleaning rod. The lever is unmarked and appears to have been nickel-plated. The trigger is plain, hinged to the plate.

> Extractor: Single hook type at bottom center of barrel.

> Firing Pin: Sliding bar type with no spring.

> Barrel: 28″ long. 0.84 in muzzle diameter, 1.12 in diameter at breech. Forearm screw lug is 8.5″ from front face of

receiver. The front sight is a small "Kentucky" type brass blade in an iron base. The rear sight is a typical iron "Kentucky" rear with an extremely small notch. The sights appear crude compared to the workmanship evidenced on the remainder of the rifle. On the bottom of the barrel under the chamber is the figure "8" and ahead of this an "0." This latter is stamped in a small spot which had been polished bright. This appears to be more of a symbol.

Stocks: Forestock and buttstock are plain varnished walnut. Butt has a curved steel rifle butt plate which may have been nickel-plated. I have not yet obtained a chamber cast from this rifle, so cannot report just what rimfire cartridge it is made for.

Here's another rimfire Peabody, but this is a military piece, not a sporter. The conformation is typical, carbine buttstocked, one band forend, plain carbine. There is no serial number to be found; however, most parts are found stamped with one alphabet letter, differing on each piece. The right side of the buttstock is stamped WC script initials in a elliptical shaped framing. It is reported these are the inspector's mark of William Chapman, who was an armory sub-inspector of purchased arms and parts from 1860 to 1864. This carbine is in .56-50 Spencer rimfire caliber and the present owner fired several Spencer cartridges in the chamber and reported they seemed to fit properly.

Now to report on two more Peabody Sporting Rifles both of which are centerfire. The first of these is numbered 116 on the front of the receiver while the barrel is numbered 5956. This takes a .45 caliber centerfire case, probably the .45 Sporting cartridge. The butt plate of this rifle is numbered '6' in the same size numerals as used on the action.

The second is a deluxe sporter, side hammer model. It is marked "PEABODY'S, PAT. JULY 22, 1862. Man'f'd. by Providence Tool Co., Prov., R.I." This has a 25 3/4" full round barrel with a forend 11" long. Hooded front sight, hood is 1" long with a large pin head sight post in it. Rear sight on barrel is much like the carbine sight, with sliding elevations, as used on Winchester Model 1892, but with no graduations. Buttstock and forend are of fancy burl walnut, checkered with the diamond pattern usually used by Providence Tool Co. Buttstock closely matches Plate 67 Page 148 of *More Single Shot Rifles*. Forend has no metal tip. Serial number is 63663 on both the barrel and receiver. Bore diameter is .453", grooves are .459-.460", 6 lands and grooves, conventional rifling.

A B.N. case made to fit the chamber and fired ten times in this chamber measures as follows:

Diameter of rim .628
Diameter under head .527
Diameter at rear of shoulder .515
Length case to start of shoulder 1.200
Length case to end of shoulder 1.275
Length case overall 1.650

This chamber appears to be cut for a paper patched bullet with at least ¼" of paper out of the mouth of case.

Now to turn our attention to the Peabody-Martini shown on *Plate Numbers 117 and 118*, the action side views of a fine Mid-Range Peabody-Martini engraved with the head of a lion on the left side (Plate 117) and that of a tiger on the right side, (Plate 118). This is a Mid-Range Creedmoor Grade rifle, serial numbered 199. It has a 30" part octagon barrel chambered for the .40-70 Peabody-Martini What Cheer cartridge.

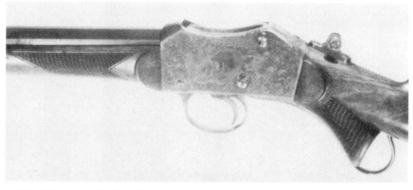

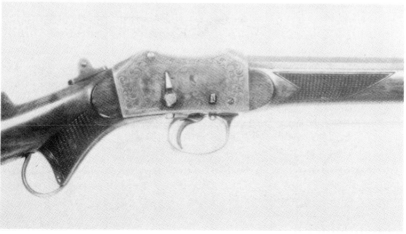

Plate Numbers 117 & 118   Peabody-Martini, Mid-Range. Note engraving on both sides of frame. (Photos: Leo Cook).

Another beautifully engraved specimen from Providence Tool Company is the deluxe Peabody-Martini displayed on *Plate Numbers 119 and 120*. They show close-ups of the action sides, while *Plate Number 121* gives a top view of this action frame, showing the engraved marking and the sharp checkering in both wood and metal. This is also a Mid-Range Peabody-Martini target rifle in the What Cheer series, as it has a straight gripped pattern stock with no pistol grip, but with a shotgun type butt plate which is generally found on the Long-Range Peabody-Martinis. The serial number is 143, marked on all the parts, including the tang sight. An extremely fine Mid-Range rifle.

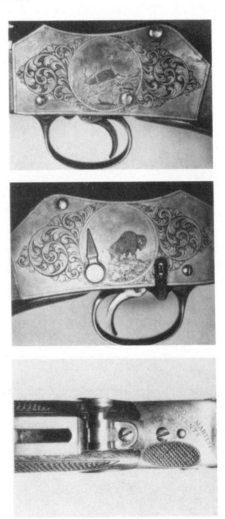

Plate Numbers 119, 120 & 121   Peabody-Martini specially engraved Mid-Range. (Photos: Ted Bacyck).

To give you more information on these interesting and finely made products from the old plant at Providence, Rhode Island, I am including photo copies of the pages of my 1881 Providence Tool Company catalogue. The catalogues issued by this company showing these products are extremely rare today. *Plate Numbers 122* to *142* inclusive show all pages of this catalogue.

THE

PEABODY-MARTINI

PATENT BREECH-LOADING

Military and Sporting Rifles

MANUFACTURED BY THE

PROVIDENCE TOOL COMPANY,

PROVIDENCE, RHODE ISLAND,

UNITED STATES OF AMERICA.

JOHN B. ANTHONY, President.

WILLIAM B. DART, Treasurer.

Plate Number 122

No. 1.

No. 2.

PROVIDENCE TOOL COMPANY'S FACTORIES.

PROVIDENCE, R. I., U. S. A.

(2)

THE PEABODY-MARTINI RIFLE.

THIS RIFLE is a combination of the Peabody and Martini patent systems, the former covering the mechanism for closing the breech, and extracting the cartridge shell, after the rifle has been fired, and the latter covering the device for igniting the cartridge. It is the adopted arm of the English and Turkish Governments, after long and exhaustive trials in competition with all the prominent breech loading rifles of the world. It has endured the test of actual experience in war during the contest between Russia and Turkey, and has obtained the highest reputation for solidity, accuracy, long range, and other desirable qualities of a military weapon. The official reports from the armies in the field, and the letters of army correspondents, unite in praise of the efficiency of the Turkish rifles, manufactured by the Providence Tool Company.

The parts composing the breech mechanism combine the greatest possible strength with simplicity of construction, and the system, in its present perfection, is the result of long and careful study to produce a rifle meeting all the requirements of military service.

Its form is compact and graceful, and the symmetry of its lines is nowhere infringed upon by unseemly projections, which, besides being offensive to the eye, are often prejudicial to the comfort of the soldier on the march, or in the performance of its necessary manipulations.

No movement of the barrel, or any other parts, except those immediately connected with the block, is required in the performance of any of its operations. These are performed in the simplest possible manner, and without in the least infringing upon the strength and durability of the rifle, which is equal, in these respects, to the best muzzle loader.

In the operation of loading, the whole movement of the block is made within the breech frame or receiver, the end of the block lever falling but a short distance from the stock. The block itself is a strong, substantial piece, and when in position for firing, is so firmly secured as to ensure its perfect safety, as has been repeatedly shown in the severe tests to which it has been subjected.

(3)

The position of the block, when it is drawn down for loading, is such as to form an inclined plane, sloping toward the breech of the barrel, and the groove in its upper surface corresponding with the bore of the barrel, facilitates the entrance of the cartridge so that it slides easily into the chamber, without the necessity even of looking to see that it is properly inserted.

The adoption of the coil main spring in place of the common gun-lock main spring, is considered a great improvement, and this opinion is confirmed by the experience of the English and Turkish troops who have been supplied with the Peabody-Martini Rifles. It has been found that, in several instances, where the coil main springs were broken, the defects were not noticed, and the springs, compressed in the blocks, worked as usual. Had such mishaps occurred to the old gun-lock main springs, the arm would have been rendered useless.

The accuracy and range of this rifle are very remarkable. The system of rifling used is that known in England as the Henry. There are seven grooves, of peculiar shape, with a sharp twist (one turn in twenty inches). After a long series of experiments, with different kinds of rifling, the English Arms Commission finally decided upon this system as giving the most satisfactory results, both with regard to accuracy and range.

The manipulations for loading and firing, are of the simplest kind. The movements are these:

First.—Throw down the block lever with considerable force, pressing with the thumb of the right hand.

Second.—Insert the cartridge.

Third.—Return lever to place, which raises the block to its proper position, when the rifle is ready for firing.

After firing, throw down the block lever with considerable force, and the empty cartridge shell is thrown out clear from the rifle, leaving the chamber ready for the insertion of another cartridge. This extraction of the cartridge shell is effected by the action of an elbow lever, which throws it out with unerring certainty, the instant the block lever is lowered. This elbow lever derives it power simply from the action of the block itself, and cannot become deranged, as its action is not dependent upon any spring, and is of such strength as to prevent the possibility of breakage or derangement by any service to which it can be subjected. If it is desired to preserve the cartridge shell for reloading, throw down the block lever with a gentle movement, and it is drawn out into the groove of the block, from whence it can readily be taken by the person firing.

(4)

For rapidity of firing, the Peabody-Martini Rifle is believed to be equal, if not superior to any other single loader, and in continuous firing, to any repeater. It cannot be fired until the block is in its proper position, so that it is impossible for accidents from premature explosion to occur. The objection to the excessive recoil of this rifle, which has been raised in some quarters, has been obviated in the arms manufactured by the Providence Tool Company, by the adoption of a different form of ammunition.

After the decision of the English Arms Commission in favor of the Peabody-Martini Rifle, and its subsequent adoption as the standard national arm, the Imperial Ottoman Government contracted with the Providence Tool Company to manufacture 600,000. The productive capacity of this Company's factories is 1000 rifles per day.

In conclusion it may be said, that wherever the Peabody-Martini Rifle has been introduced, its superior qualities of safety, strength, simplicity, easy manipulation, accuracy and long range, have been fully conceded.

Providence, June 1st, 1878.

INTERNATIONAL EXHIBITION.

PHILADELPHIA, 1876.

REPORT ON AWARDS.

"As a Military Gun, combining Strength, Simplicity,
High Quality of Workmanship,
Ease of Manipulation, with Accuracy and Rapidity of Fire;
Using a Central Fire Metallic Cartridge,
and Ejecting the Discharged Shell
Unfailingly."

(5)

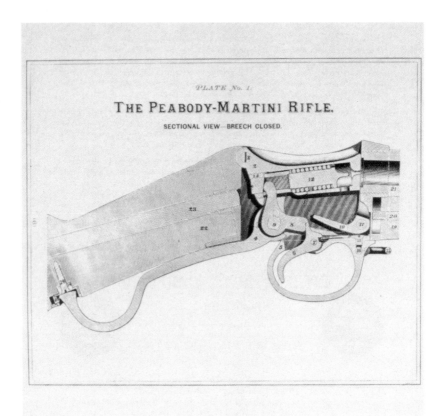

PLATE No. 1.

THE PEABODY-MARTINI RIFLE.

SECTIONAL VIEW—BREECH CLOSED.

Explanation of Plate No. 1.

Figure No. 1. Receiver, or Breech Frame.
" " 2. Block.
" " 3. Block Axis Pin.
" " 4. Lever.
" " 5. Trigger Guard.
" " 6. Trigger.
" " 7. Trigger Axis Screw.
" " 8. Tumbler.
" " 9. Indicator.
" " 10. Extractor.
" " 11. Extractor Axis Screw.
" " 12. Striker.
" " 13. Coil Main Spring.
" " 14. Stop Nut.
" " 15. Trigger Guard Swivel.
" " 16. Trigger Guard Swivel Screw.
" " 17. Trigger Spring.
" " 18. Trigger Spring Screw.
" " 19. Tip Stock.
" " 20. Cleaning Rod.
" " 21. Barrel.
" " 22. Butt Stock.
" " 23. Butt Bolt.
" " 24. Block Lever Catch.
" " 25. Block Lever Catch Spring.
" " 26. Block Lever Catch Screw.

(7)

PLATE No. 2.

THE PEABODY-MARTINI RIFLE.

SECTIONAL VIEW—BREECH OPEN.

Explanation of Plate No. 2.

Figure No. 1. Receiver, or Breech Frame.
" " 2. Block.
" " 3. Block Axis Pin.
" " 4. Lever.
" " 5. Trigger Guard.
" " 6. Trigger.
" " 7. Trigger Axis Screw.
" " 8. Tumbler.
" " 9. Indicator.
" " 10. Extractor.
" " 11. Extractor Axis Screw.
" " 12. Striker.
" " 13. Coil Main Spring.
" " 14. Stop Nut.
" " 15. Trigger Guard Swivel.
" " 16. Trigger Guard Swivel Screw.
" " 17. Trigger Spring.
" " 18. Trigger Spring Screw.
" " 19. Tip Stock.
" " 20. Cleaning Rod.
" " 21. Barrel.
" " 22. Butt Stock.
" " 23. Butt Bolt.
" " 24. Block Lever Catch.
" " 25. Block Lever Catch Spring.
" " 26. Block Lever Catch Screw.

Explanation of Plate No. 3.

Figure No. 1. Receiver, or Breech Frame.
" " 2. Block.
" " 3. Block Axis Pin.
" " 4. Lever.
" " 5. Trigger Guard.
" " 6. Trigger.
" " 7. Trigger Axis Screw.
" " 8. Tumbler.
" " 9. Indicator.
" " 10. Extractor.
" " 11. Extractor Axis Screw.
" " 14. Stop Nut.
" " 15. Trigger Guard Swivel.
" " 16. Trigger Guard Swivel Screw.
" " 19. Tip Stock.
" " 21. Barrel.
" " 22. Butt Stock.

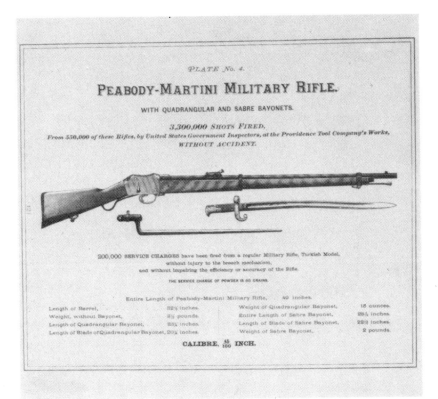

PLATE No. 4.

PEABODY-MARTINI MILITARY RIFLE.

WITH QUADRANGULAR AND SABRE BAYONETS.

3,300,000 SHOTS FIRED,
From 550,000 of these Rifles, by United States Government Inspectors, at the Providence Tool Company's Works,
WITHOUT ACCIDENT.

200,000 SERVICE CHARGES have been fired from a regular Military Rifle, Turkish Model,
without injury to the breech mechanism,
and without impairing the efficiency or accuracy of the Rifle.

THE SERVICE CHARGE OF POWDER IS 85 GRAINS.

Entire Length of Peabody-Martini Military Rifle,   40 inches.

Length of Barrel,	32¼ inches.	Weight of Quadrangular Bayonet,	18 ounces.
Weight, without Bayonet,	8¾ pounds.	Entire Length of Sabre Bayonet,	28½ inches.
Length of Quadrangular Bayonet,	23½ inches.	Length of Blade of Sabre Bayonet,	22½ inches.
Length of Blade of Quadrangular Bayonet,	20¼ inches.	Weight of Sabre Bayonet,	2 pounds.

CALIBRE, $\frac{45}{100}$ INCH.

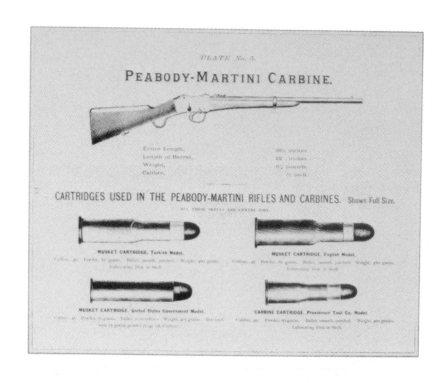

PLATE No. 5.

PEABODY-MARTINI CARBINE.

Entire Length,	38½ inches.
Length of Barrel,	22 inches.
Weight,	6½ pounds.
Calibre,	.45 inch.

CARTRIDGES USED IN THE PEABODY-MARTINI RIFLES AND CARBINES. Shown Full Size.

MUSKET CARTRIDGE, Turkish Model.

MUSKET CARTRIDGE, English Model.

MUSKET CARTRIDGE, United States Government Model.

CARBINE CARTRIDGE, Providence Tool Co. Model.

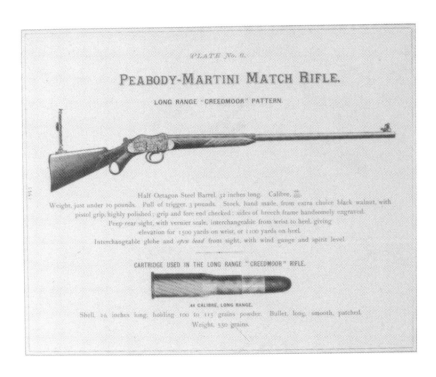

PLATE No. 6.

PEABODY-MARTINI MATCH RIFLE.

LONG RANGE "CREEDMOOR" PATTERN.

Half-Octagon Steel Barrel, 32 inches long. Calibre, $\frac{22}{100}$.
Weight, just under 10 pounds. Pull of trigger, 3 pounds. Stock, hand made, from extra choice black walnut, with
pistol grip, highly polished; grip and fore end checked; sides of breech frame handsomely engraved.
Peep-rear sight, with vernier scale, interchangeable from wrist to heel, giving
elevation for 1500 yards on wrist, or 1100 yards on heel.
Interchangeable globe and *open bead* front sight, with wind gauge and spirit level.

CARTRIDGE USED IN THE LONG RANGE "CREEDMOOR" RIFLE.

44 CALIBRE, LONG RANGE.

Shell, 2½ inches long, holding 100 to 115 grains powder. Bullet, long, smooth, patched.
Weight, 550 grains.

PLATE No. 7.

PEABODY-MARTINI HUNTING AND SPORTING RIFLE.

"KILL DEER" PATTERN.

Designed for use on the Plains, for Hunting Large Game, or for off-hand Practice

AT 100 TO 500 YARDS.

Half Octagon Steel Barrel, 28 inches long. Calibre, $\frac{45}{100}$. Weight of rifle, 8 to 9 pounds. Pull of trigger, 3 pounds.
Stock, hand made, from first class black walnut. Broad flat butt-plate. Interchangeable
globe and peep and open sights.

SIGHTS CAN BE CHANGED WHILE THE GAME IS IN VIEW.

CARTRIDGE USED IN THE "KILL DEER" RIFLE.

CALIBRE .45.

This cartridge is the same model as used by the U. S. Government in its Military Rifles and Carbines.
Powder, 70 grains. Bullet, 3 cannelures. Weight, 405 grains.

TARGETS

MADE WITH A

PEABODY-MARTINI MILITARY RIFLE.

TURKISH MODEL.

By United States Inspector OLDHAM, at Bridgeport, Conn., June 24, 1877, in presence of
General TEVFIK PASHA, Delegate of the Imperial Ottoman Government,
charged with the supervision of arms and ammunition,
manufactured in this country for that
Government.

Twenty consecutive shots, at 500 metres.   Diameter of bull's-eye, 22 inches.

Fifteen consecutive shots, at 900 metres.   Diameter of bull's-eye, 36 inches.

(16)

DIRECTIONS

DISMOUNTING AND ASSEMBLING BREECH-ACTION.

NUMBERS REFER TO PLATE NO. 1, ON PAGE 6.

TO DISMOUNT BODY No. 1.

1. Push out Block Axis-pin No. 3.
2. Open the Breech, and with the thumb press with force on front end of Block No. 2, and at the same time raise Lever No. 4.
3. Turn Keeper-screw so as to allow Indicator No. 9 to be pushed out.
4. Take out Extractor Axis-screw No. 11. The parts now are all disengaged.

TO ASSEMBLE BODY No. 1.

1. Put Lever No. 4 back to its place in assembled Guard No. 5, and insert both in Body No. 1; Drop in Extractor No. 10, and turn in Extractor Axis-screw No. 11.
2. Put Tumbler No. 8 in place, and put in Indicator No. 9, point upright, and secure Keeper-screw.
3. With the right hand raise the Lever No. 4 so as to touch the Lever Catch No. 24, then with the first finger pull the Trigger No. 6 back, and with the thumb push the Indicator No. 9 forward, and drop in the assembled Block No. 2, the front end entering first ; Apply a little force to back end of Block with the left hand, moving the Lever a little at the same time with the right hand, and the Block will drop into place.
4. Insert Block Axis-pin No. 3.

TO DISMOUNT GUARD No. 5.

1. Take out Trigger Spring Screw No. 18, relieving Trigger Spring No. 17.
2. Take out Trigger Axis-screw No. 7, relieving Trigger No. 6.

TO ASSEMBLE GUARD No. 5.

1. Hold Trigger No. 6 in place, and turn in Trigger Axis-screw No. 7.
2. Restore Trigger Spring No. 17, and turn in Trigger Spring Screw No. 18. (The parts are now ready to be attached to the Body No. 1.)

TO DISMOUNT BLOCK No. 2.

Turn Keeper-screw on end of Block No. 2, and take out Stop-nut No. 14. The Striker No. 12 and Coil Spring No. 13, will then drop out.

TO ASSEMBLE BLOCK No. 2.

Restore Striker No. 12 and Coil Spring No. 13 to place, turn in Stop-nut No. 14 and turn Keeper-screw to secure it.

NOTE.—The Striker No. 12 has a rectangular slot near one end. This slot is longer on one side than on the other. The long side should be so placed as to admit end of Tumbler No. 8, freely.

After a little practice the Breech-Action can be assembled in detail in three minutes.

(7)

Re-Loading Tools.

DIRECTIONS FOR RE-LOADING CENTRAL FIRE CARTRIDGE SHELLS, ANY CALIBRE, SPORTING AND MILITARY.

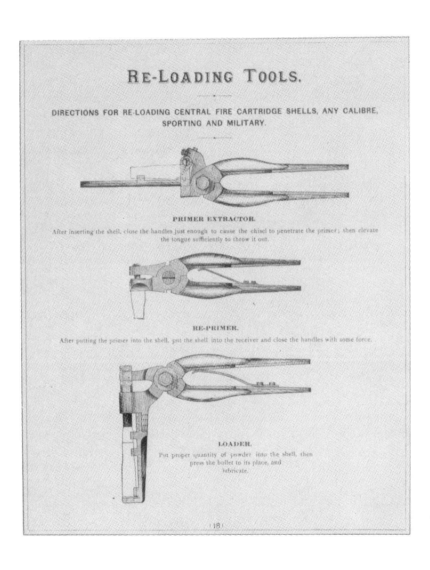

PRIMER EXTRACTOR.

After inserting the shell, close the handles just enough to cause the chisel to penetrate the primer; then elevate the tongue sufficiently to throw it out.

RE-PRIMER.

After putting the primer into the shell, put the shell into the receiver and close the handles with some force.

LOADER.

Put proper quantity of powder into the shell, then press the bullet to its place, and lubricate.

(18)

Parties wishing prices and terms of sale, of the

PEABODY-MARTINI RIFLES,

CARTRIDGES, &c.

*Can obtain same by applying directly to the Providence Tool Company,
or its authorized Agents.*

(19)

The
Providence Tool Company

ARE ALSO MANUFACTURERS OF

SHIP CHANDLERY ☞ MARINE HARDWARE,

Including Norcross' Patent Tackle Blocks, and Special Blocks
for Power Hoisting.

HEAVY HARDWARE ☞ R. R. SUPPLIES,

Including Nuts, Washers, Chain Links, Bolt Ends, Turn-Buckles,
Threshing Machine Teeth, &c. &c.

THE "HOUSEHOLD" SEWING MACHINE,

For Family and Light Manufacturing Purposes,
and the

KEATS LOCK-STITCH SEWING MACHINE,

For all kinds of Leather Work, making a Lock Stitch with two
threads, both sides alike, with any kind
of hard wax.

(20)

At least one specimen of the Peabody-Wessely rifle has turned up recently. This rare model was mentioned in *Boys' Rifles* and the specimen is exactly like the phamphlet illustrations showed. It is a 30″ barrel military stocked, in caliber .42 Russian. Forend has two bands, blued barrel, and case hardened receiver. There are no markings whatsoever on the arm and we believe it to be a handmade tool room model. It is beautifully made and finished. The action is very compact and neat, just a fraction of an inch longer than the hammer model made in .43 caliber for the State of Connecticut.

A beautifully engraved Peabody-Martini rifle is shown in the action-side engraving depicted on *Plate Numbers 143 and 144*. This is a Mid-Range, What Cheer Grade specially engraved. The serial number is 208, on the frame, barrel, stock, sights, etc. Barrel is marked on the flat of the muzzle (the usual place) ".40 Cal. 70 Grs." Part octagon, part round barrel, 30 inches long. Marked "Manufactured by the Providence Tool Co., Providence, R.I., U.S.A." On the underside of trigger guard "Peabody & Martini Patents."

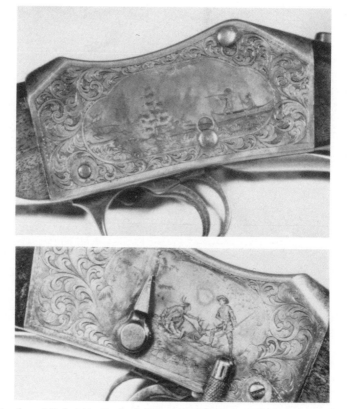

Plate Numbers 143 & 144   Peabody-Martini Mid-Range, What Cheer grade. Note the engraving depicts a hunter's chase and kill. (Photos: Jack Appel).

The engraving is extremely well done and it will bear close examination with a powerful magnifying glass. The motif of the engraving is quite obvious in these close-up photographs of the frame. The old Providence Tool Company had extremely able engraver-artists working on some of their Peabody-Martinis as the rifles themselves testify. It is odd that it is so very difficult today to learn who actually did this work and more about them, since the engravers who worked on early Colt revolvers and Winchester rifle receivers have been well covered by several researchers.

Now, on *Plate Numbers 145 and 146*, is depicted another deluxe example of engraving supplied by Providence Tool Co. on their fine rifles.

This rifle frame is that of a Long-Range Creedmoor grade rifle which is in .44-100 What Cheer caliber. The serial number of this fine piece is 93.

Plate Numbers 145 & 146 Peabody-Martini Long-Range Creedmoor, .44-100 What Cheer caliber. (Photos: Edward Haight.)

VIII

Browning and Winchester

We have just a few additional notes on the single shot Brownings and Winchesters to communicate. The factory issue models of Winchester and Sharps rifles have been covered from time to time in the past three books so there isn't too much to add at this time.

Starting with the granddaddy of the Winchester, the J. M. Browning patent of 1879, there have been called to my attention some which differ a bit from the usual Browning single shot, and are certainly worth mentioning.

First is a Browning single shot which was listed in *More Single Shot Rifles*, page 117. The rifle was described at that time as being in .50-95 Sharps caliber, however, later close observation rules that out. It is apparently chambered for the 1870's service cartridge, the .50-70 Gov't. I have not received a chamber cast of this rifle and am not positive about the actual case used, but it is the only .50 caliber Browning to come to light.

A full length illustration of the rifle in question is shown on *Plate Number 147* and a close-up of the action is on *Plate Number 148*. The serial number of 196 is plainly seen on the right rear flat of the barrel. This serial number is also stamped on top of the barrel, which is also marked '50'. There are no other markings on the gun, which is unusual in itself. Generally they are plainly marked with the maker's name and address.

As I mentioned in *Volume Two*, the authentication of the genuineness of this rifle came through Mr. W. F. Vickery, the Idaho gunsmith, from Mr. Val Browning.

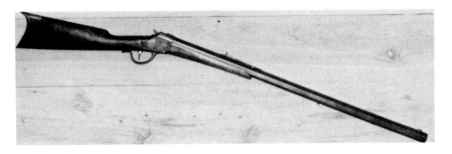

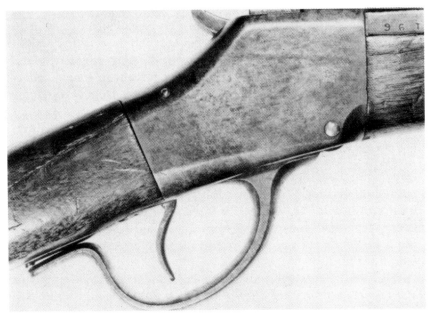

Plate Numbers 147 & 148   The .50 caliber John M. Browning Rifle with close-up of the ultra-plain breech section. (Photos: Dr. R. L. Moore).

Another John Browning single shot rifle is shown on *Plate Number 149*, and this one has a frame contour which is unusual. It does not conform to practically any of the others in existence today. The photo isn't as good as I would like, but the frame outlines show up well and that is what we are discussing. The hammer of this piece is also hung or slung (whichever you prefer) lower in the frame than is usual. This rifle is serial numbered 123 and top of the barrel is stamped "J. M. Browning, Ogden, U.T." Also on top of the barrel is "40-100 C70G. 123," which deciphers to 40 caliber, 70 grains, serial number, of course, being the 123.

145

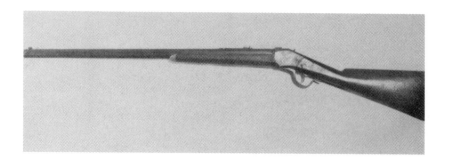

Plate Number 149   Browning Single Shot Rifle. (Photo: Rex O. Smith).

I will mention one more Browning single shot which is also different from the usual plain pattern. This rifle, which turned up in California, is also in .40-70 S.S. caliber and is a rather deluxe version, being a pistol grip stock rifle with the usual rifle butt plate. The pistol grip is checkered, (but not the forend) in a professional manner. The serial number of '509' appears on the front of the frame and on the top of barrel, just ahead of the action frame ring. In front of the rear sight is marked "BROWNING BROS., OGDEN, UTAH, U.S.A." in back of the rear sight is marked "Pat. Oct., 7, '79. . . .40-70." The barrel is 30¼" long, full octagon with a silver blade insert front sight. Rear sight is the usual open Buckhorn pattern used on most of these rifles. What makes this rifle different and worth noting is the fact that the top of receiver is made with three flats, like much later Winchester Model 1885 actions; but, these three flats are milled into a scalloped pattern with the opening of these scallops facing the rear of the frame.

With this rifle, to the present owner, came a combination mould and loading tool marked .40-70. Bullets from this mould weigh 317 grains. This is a full folding mould and repriming tool, similar to that generally accompanying Maynard rifles, but also used by others. Also in the assortment, were a lead ladle marked "XXX ORNE & CO" (with first portion of the name unreadable), a bar of lead stamped "Bogue Lead Co., Denver," a small quantity of non-headstamped cartridge cases and a box of Winchester primers.

Winchester Notes

Turning now to the principal descendent of the J. M. Browning, the Winchester; and, especially well known to the single shot collector, the Model 1885 single-shot.

On *Plate Numbers 150 and 151*, two close-up views of the engraving appearing on a fine Winchester hi-side wall Scheutzen rifle. This rifle is .32-40 caliber with a #4 part octagon barrel. It is, as

146

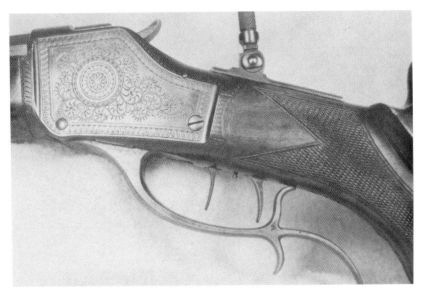

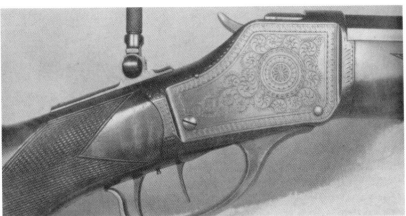

Plate Numbers 150 & 151   Winchester High-side wall, showing superb engraving.
(Photos: Brian Kent).

you see, in the photo a full Scheutzen pattern rifle with double
Scheutzen set Winchester triggers, spur finger lever and pistol grip
stock with the Helm pattern butt plate. Hi-side wall rifles engraved
by Winchester at their factory are so scarce we like to mention every
one we see. This rifle has a serial number of 102596. There is no palm
rest on the rifle. The Lyman tang sight on the rifle was placed there
by Winchester according to verification.

For those wishing to pursue the many differences in the
Winchester single shot actions, I refer you to my two issue article on
these which appeared in the June and July, 1967 issues of *Guns
Magazine*, published by Publishers Development Corp., 591 Camino
de la Reina, Suite 200, San Diego, Ca. 92108.

IX

Some Maynard Rifle Notes

I have just a very few additions to the Maynard chapters of the previous three books.

First a mention of a rifle with perhaps the heaviest original barrel around. This is serial numbered 26880. It is an 1873 rifle, with a round barrel measuring 1.585 inches at the breech and 1.520 inches at the muzzle. This barrel may have been reblued, but if so, it was many years ago and finish has turned brown. Most of the case colors have disappeared from the frame, but there aren't too many Maynards around with much color left in this part. The buttstock is of burl walnut with a brass butt plate, old nickel finish, turned quite dull. There is an old telescopic sight mounted on the barrel and; while it is unmarked, it, and the mounts appear to be of Malcolm manufacture. The front mount is of the usual windage adjustment as made by Malcolm, while the elevation adjustment is in the rear mount. This rifle came in a very old wood case, lined with green velvet. There is a 50 case capacity wooden block in the case which is for the .40-70 cartridges.

In *Boys' Rifles*, page 502, there was shown a fine Maynard Number 14 Creedmoor rifle. Another Creedmoor has turned up since then and it is apparently another number 14 with a 32" barrel for the .44-100 cartridge; but, this takes the '82 style cartridge case since this latter rifle is an 1882 model. It has the shotgun buttstock of the '73 pattern as well as the pistol grip knob built on the rear of the finger lever. This rifle lacks the thumb support usually mounted just immediately to the rear of the tang sight. The sight hole spacing of this tang is different from other Maynards examined so far, inasmuch as the hole spacing here is 1½ " center to center of screw holes.

As I mentioned in *Boys' Rifles* in the table on tang sights (Page 589), the usual and regular hole spacing of the Maynard top tangs is 7/8" center to center of holes. Most of these sights, both the 1865 tang and the 1873 and 1882 tang sights have a base approximately 1¼ " long, held on with the two screws on 7/8" or 29/32" centers. There is also a spring plunger coming up from the tang through this base to hold the sight in position, either erect or in the folded position.

Another base rarely seen is one which is thicker than the above regular base. This is about 3/16" thick, similar in appearance to the regular Ballard base and about 1 3/4" long and 1/2" wide. This base usually has the same 7/8" hole spacing as the more common base. One such sight base observed on a .32-35 1882 Model 16 Maynard rifle has the usual rack and pinion actuated sight staff mounted on it. This staff is held erect by a spring on the underside of the base, like the Ballard sights. The top tang of this particular rifle is also drilled for the regular Maynard base-holding screws on 7/8" centers, and also for the spring plunger. I am not ruling out the possibility that the Maynard rack and pinion staff was fitted to a Ballard sight base and this mounted on this tang. However, to complicate this even more, I have seen two or three other Maynard staffs on other bases similar to the one described above.

I am still working on the puzzle of the Maynard .35-55-170 Express cartridge. I have more reports of, and more chamber casts from, actual barrels which the owners believe might be chambered for this cartridge. I will tabulate these dimensions on a table at the end of this chapter.

I will mention one report which will not be entered in this table, and say here, it is an opinion which was advanced to me some years ago. The informant was quoting from an article published in *The Rifle* in September 1886, concerning the guns used by Major Charles W. Hinman, a well known and respected rifleman. Mr. Hinman first used Long-Range Rifles. Let me quote from that issue of *The Rifle*.

"The portability of the Maynard attracted Mr. Hinman's attention, and as the barrel of this arm could be easily detached and the rifle packed in a trunk of very small compass, he laid aside his Kirkwood rifle and adopted the Maynard. He first chose a .40 caliber barrel and later a .35 caliber, and the arm was made up according to his ideas of correctness . . . and in place of the Everlasting shell, a thin solid-head Remington shell is used which in his .35 caliber barrels, are chambered for holding 60 grains of powder . . . a bullet weighing 330 grains was formerly used, but recently he adopted one weighing 250 grains, which is cast by himself and unswaged." Now according to the dates given in the article, this was *before* 1882. The Maynards he may have used could have been the .38-50 caliber Maynard; or, possibly, .35-40 specially chambered to accept *larger* capacity shells.

Later on, possibly, he obtained a Maynard .35-55-170 barrel, this could easily have transpired before the article in the 1886 issue of *The Rifle*. The Maynard Express .35-55-170 case was more than likely a thin walled, solid head case developed for the 1882 rifle, but certainly *after* 1882.

It's not difficult to get five more grains of black powder in a shell whose normal capacity was 55 grains. Also, since Mr. Hinman cast his own bullets and did not swage them, this sounds very much like he used heavier paper patched bullets, probably seated out a trifle farther in the mouth of the case to accommodate the slight extra powder charge. The 330 grains weight bullets mentioned as being used by him were no doubt for his .40 caliber rifles, before he went to the .35 calibers. The 330 grains bullet was commonly used in many .38 and .40 caliber rifles.

All this conjecture gets us nowhere in the labyrinth of the Maynard .35 Express cartridge. I only mention it to show attempts to attack the problem from all angles. In the Massachusetts Arms Company catalogue for 1888, at the top of page 26 under "Shells for the Maynard" is listed—"Solid Head Shells' 35 caliber 55 grains (Remington) per hundred. . . . $3.50." On page 27, under cartridges is listed: ".35-55-170 per 100. . . . .$5.00." Again quoting from this catalogue, page 24 shows: "List of Prices, Rifle Barrels, 28, 30 or 32 inch .35 caliber 55 grains. . . . .$12.00." This catalogue does give Remington credit for making these .35 Express shells for them, and very possibly most of the sizes used by the Maynards could have been made by this same manufacturer.

From the foregoing, and from what was written in the last two books, I feel it is reasonable and safe to say the Maynard .35-55-170 Express had these loading specifications of .35 caliber, 55 grains of black powder; and, since it was an Express cartridge, a naked grooved, lubricated bullet weighing 170 grains. No rifleman was forced to load it this way of course, he could boost the charge up somewhat and use heavier grooved or paper patched bullets if he preferred. Certainly, a longer slug, paper patched, would weigh more than the standard 170 grain grooved bullet.

150

Plate Number 152 shows some Maynard cartridges and cases, not the .55 Express, unfortunately. Perhaps this will come along later. I have included a .35 Wesson Paper Patch bullet cartridge, however.

Explanation of *Plate 152* is as follows, left to right:

    Head of .35-40 Maynard case
          .35-40 Maynard case erected
          .35-40 Maynard loaded cartridge
          .35 Wesson cartridge.

The following page gives the specifications of two rifles surveyed which are more than likely chambered for our .35-55-170 Maynard Express Cartridge.

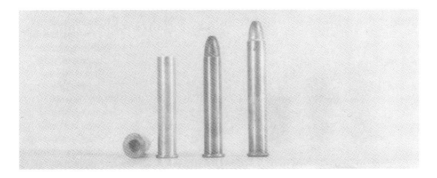

Plate Number 152   Maynard & Wesson Cartridges.

MAYNARD CHAMBER SURVEY FOR .35-55-170 EXPRESS CARTRIDGE

RIFLE	RIM DIA.	UNDER RIM	MOUTH DIA.	BULLET	CASE LENGTH	GROOVES	REMARKS
Maynard '82 Rifle (Nebraska)		.458"	.381"		2.200- 2 3/16"	.360- .361"	Rifle fired with .303 British cases and reloaded with 55 gr. blackpowder. This fills fire-formed case to with-in 3/16" of mouth. 170 gr. bullet can be seated enough to cover all grooves in slug. From a mea-sured chamber cast.
Maynard '82 Rifle (Texas)		.457	.381- .383"		2 3/16"- 2 7/32"	.360"	This rifle came with 20 cases made by A. O. Niedner from .30-40 brass after the necked section of the original case had been trimmed off. These were made for a former owner of this rifle. These dimensions are from a chamber cast.
This is a loaded un-known cart-ridge.	.505"	.402"	.398"	.378"	2 1/32"		This cartridge was suggested as being the .35-55-170 May-nard Express, but seems too far from above two chamber casts to qualify. Too small at head and too short over-all.

It would appear from the above measured chamber casts, one from a rifle owned in Nebraska, the other in a collection in Texas, that these should be considered fairly correct to qualify for our Maynard Express. These two rifles have come to my attention since *Volume Three Boys Single Shot Rifles* was published.

I am sure there are other Model 1882 Maynard rifles around here and there in collections which are also chambered for the .35-55-170 cartridge, but this pair are the only ones meeting the called-for specifications we've seen. It is not often one meets a collector who is interested enough to cast a chamber in his rifle, or rifles, and send it to me. When this does happen, it is possible to determine fairly accurately just what the piece was made to use in the way of cartridges.

X

More Interesting Remingtons

I wish to call to your attention some more variations and additional material which has come to light on Remington single shot rifles. There was a report of an engraved number 7 Remington rolling block rifle some time back. The following information was furnished by the owner of the piece at that time, but I was never able to obtain a good photograph and more exact details, so am not showing the actual rifle. The rifle may not be, possibly is not, factory engraved. It has a .22 Long Rifle rimfire barrel marked "Remington Arms Co., Ilion, N.Y., U.S.A."—"22 L.R." in front of forestock on underside of the barrel, and under the forestock it is marked "22 L.R. 339." Serial number on the action is NT 300339, and marked under the butt plate on the wood is—"A. O. Niedner, Malden, Mass."

It has no slot for front or rear sights in the barrel but has a small diameter Malcolm telescopic sight on this barrel. The frame is completely engraved similar to the one shown on Plate 43, top rifle, in *More Single Shot Rifles*. Only on a smaller scale, of course. There is some engraving also on the barrel.

Here is a Remington No. 1 Rolling Block system rifle, with an octagon topped receiver ring which retains about 90 percent of the case colors, though these are fading somewhat. The extractor is the sliding type along the barrel. The serial number is in the 2900 range marked on lower tang, barrel and on butt plate, buttstock, forearm and tip. The buttstock is the straight grip type with a curved steel butt plate. Most of the original finish is still on the butt plate and the stock. The forearm is the splinter standard style with a case hardened steel tip. The sights consist of a small globe front, open middle barrel sight, this with an aperature, also. Barrel is 26" full octagon, measures 1.020" across flats at the muzzle and 1.080" at the breech. Bore and chamber are near perfect, barrel retains 90 percent of the original blue.

Now we come to the unusual part, that is the cartridge this rifle is chambered for. On the bottom of the barrel, ahead of the forearm wood it is stamped "44 CTGE." and on underside of barrel, beneath the forearm "44-60W." The chamber appears to be original and unaltered. A .44-40 WCF cartridge will not enter this chamber so it could not have been rechambered from that. The dimensions of the chamber case are as follows: Diameter of rim .570", diameter ahead of rim .467", diameter at mouth of shell .465". Length under the head is 2.125" and overall length of the cast is 2.205". There is a gradual tapered throat that is .300" long. The bore diameter taken from a slug forced through the barrel is .429". The twist of the rifling is 1 in 26". This case is nearly straight with no neck, of course.

The owner recently fire-formed some .30-40 Krag cases and used a 232 grain cast bullet. After trimming the cases, the rifle turned in respectable 2.5" 5 shot groups at 100 yards. Load used was 22 grains of 4227. Lube on the cast bullets was 65 percent beeswax and 35 percent tallow. More on this chamber later.

I recently examined a Remington Number Two Rolling Block action which is unusual. At least, it is unusual as far as I am concerned, never having seen one just like it before.

One 'expert' who examined this action before I did, pronounced it 'a fake, they were never made that way.'

I did look this action over and found the breech block is milled for the rotary type extractor actuator. An extractor-like cam engages an ear on the sliding side of the barrel (or conventional) extractor which rotates this cam counter-clockwise on opening the breech. This cam ear engages the firing pin retractor, thus withdrawing the firing pin.

The mechanism, as described, is not a modification of an existing original Remington breech block; for if it were, the hole for the firing pin retainer pin would show. (The closing of the original pin hole would of course be evident.) The only possibility of this retractor mechanism not being original to this particular action, would have been for the remodeler to obtain a new, (unfinished perhaps) breech block and installed his own modification of a firing pin retractor. The breech block appears original to the frame.

154

Perhaps you have encountered a Remington Number Two with a firing pin retractor such as this, and have dismissed it as being a gunsmith alteration. You could be right in this assumption, and I for one would not refute it; but, we must remember that the men who made these are gone now, and since there are no factory records covering such minor details of construction, who can say they were *not* made like this.

I have a report of a Remington Creedmoor very similar to the one illustrated on page 145, figure L, in *Single Shot Rifles*. This piece has a part octagon, part round barrel instead of the full round one shown in that illustration. This barrel is 34" long, five lands and five grooves and is marked on the top flat, "E. Remington & Sons, Ilion, New York"; and, ahead of the forend, on bottom of the barrel is "44S." The groove diameter of this barrel is .452-453." The chamber is for a bottle necked case of the following dimensions: Diameter of rim .640", diameter under head .525", diameter of base of neck .515", diameter of neck at rear is .473" and diameter at front neck is .470". The neck shoulder has a 10° angle. Length under head to start, or rear, of shoulder is 1 5/8" and length overall under head is 2 7/16". This is evidently chambered for the Remington Special Creedmoor case, 2 7/16" bottle neck. Even though stamped "44S" this was *mainly* a Remington case instead of being a Sharps. Sharps may have used it to some extent, perhaps even originated it, but all I have seen chambered for it have been Remingtons. The marking of "44S" seen on many barrels made by Remington does not always indicate just which case that barrel was made for. Did they have just one .44 caliber stamp?

This particular rifle is of the Long-Range pattern with a pistol gripped, shotgun buttstock and the usual Remington vernier tang tall sight. The bore diameter of a true .45 caliber is somewhat unusual, of course; but, nothing to be excited about, as sometimes there is almost no difference between the .44 and .45 borings of barrels in all the older Long-Range rifles, whether made by Remington, Sharps or Ballard.

Let's introduce a Remington-Hepburn Mid-Range rifle which has the owner puzzled . . . and, I might add, me, too! The rifle, serial number 6665, is in .40-70 2½" Sharps Straight. Nothing unusual about that of course, that was a popular cartridge and many Hepburns are seen chambered for it. The barrel is cut five lands and grooves. The grooves are twice as wide as the lands and the twist is right hand. This rifle is equipped with two sets of sights. The muzzle end of the barrel has two sets of dovetail slots for a Wind Gauge and also for a hunting sight. The tang sight is a plain adjustment long range. It is 5 3/4" long from the bottom of the base to the top of staff. The graduations are from 0 to 5. This rear sight is like Number 18 on Page 29 *Single Shot Rifles*. These sights have a rather small diameter, flat faced screw-in disc which has the peep for aiming. The rifle has the usual long pistol grip commonly seen on the Hepburn and has a Swiss, or offhand, buttplate.

Now for the puzzling part: Under the forearm the barrel is marked "S B FREUND SGT." These stampings seem to be old and the barrel gives no sign of being reblued. These letters were apparently put on the barrel with individual letter stamps, not a one piece stamp. The S's are upside down and the 'E' is over stamped, obviously the first letter was incorrect and the E stamped over it. I would guess this is the name of a previous owner, put on the barrel by himself.

Another offhand Remington, a Number 2 rolling block model, is illustrated on *Plate Number 153*. A fine little rifle in .25-20 Single Shot caliber. It has a 25 3/4" part octagon barrel. The action frame, offhand butt plate and the forearm tip are nickel-plated. The European walnut stocks just have the pistol grip area checkered; the forearm is plain, no checkering. The barrel has a spirit level, Wind Gauge front sight (missing in the photo) and a short range vernier tang rear sight. This rifle is all original and has the serial number of 18689.

From the collection of the premier Remington rifle collector, Jack Appel, we show many very unusual and interesting pieces.

The first of these is the Remington Vest Pocket Split Breech rifle shown on *Plate Number 154*. This is quite rare and is based on the split breech vest pocket frame with a long barrel and a folding detachable stock. This has a 22½" barrel numbered 4996, the grip frame being numbered 4773.

Plate Number 153   Remington Offhand Number 2 Rifle. (Photo: Leo Cook).

156

Next, the extremely rare Geiger Patent Rifle. This may possibly be the only specimen of this patent in rifle form. This piece is .58 rimfire caliber. It was only after Geiger went to England to have his rifle produced, that Remington sent a buyer there to purchase his patent. This Geiger Patent, plus the Rider Patent, became Remington's famous rolling block action.

Please refer tc Page 91, *More Single Shot Rifles* to see the J. Rider Patent, Pat'd. Jan. 3, 1865. *Plate Numbers 155 and 155A* show the copy of the original Geiger patent drawing and a photo of the rifle. *Plate Numbers 156 and 157* illustrate both sides of the action portion of a .50-70 caliber New York State Rifle. These rifles were Creedmoor shooting prizes. Documented in *"National Rifle Association Annual Report 1876"* published in 1877. On pages 43 to 61: "1st, Gold and Silver mounted military rifle presented by E. Remington & Sons."

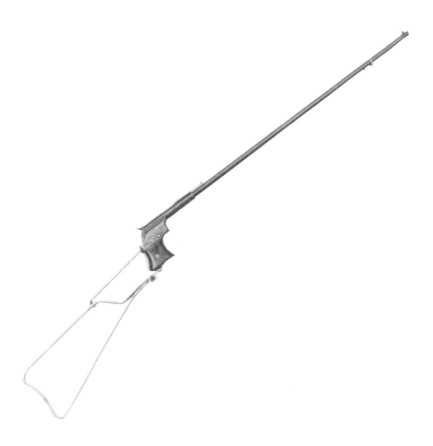

Plate Number 154   Remington Split Breech Pocket Rifle. (Photo: Jack Appel).

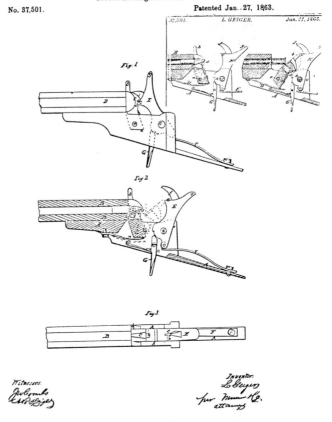

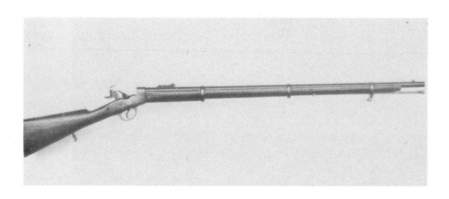

Plate Numbers 155 & 155A The Geiger Patent Drawing and a Leonard Geiger patent Rifle. (Photos: Jack Appel).

158

Plate Numbers 156 & 157   (Photos: Jack Appel).

Another fine Military Model Rifle is shown on *Plate Numbers 158 and 159*. This rifle, serial number 12942, has a 36″ barrel for the .50-70 cartridge. Probably a presentation model, beautifully engraved between the three barrel bands. Bands and sight also engraved. The barrel and butt plate nickel-plated. Bands and sight were probably gold-plated. On the swivels: "Pat'd. Feb. 11th, 1869." Serial number 12942 on both inside tangs. "B" on barrel bands. "#3" on inside tang and on stock. On top tang is "Remingtons. Ilion, N.Y., U.S.A. Pat'd. May 3rd, Nov. 15th, 1864, Apr. 17, 1868, Aug. 27, 1867, Nov. 7th, 1871."

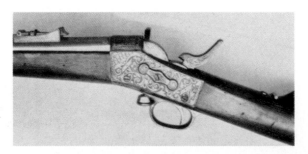

Plate Numbers 158 & 159   Fine engraved Remington Rolling Block Military Rifle. (Photos: Jack Appel).

Another deluxe rolling block is shown on *Plate Numbers 160 and 161*. This, too, is a New York State Military Model Rifle. As with all New York State Models, the hammer goes to safety notch after loading and closing the rolling block. This rifle, caliber .50-70 is beautifully engraved on entire action frame, trigger guard, block, etc. Also on top of barrel between barrel bands, all screws, buttplate, etc. Markings on bands: "Leon Backer Oct. 10, 1873." On top tang is stamped: "Remingtons, Ilion, N.Y., U.S.A. Pat'd. May 3rd, Nov. 15th, 1864, Apr. 17, 1868, Aug. 27, 1867, Nov. 7th, 1871." Serial number is 6936. Leon Backer was given his rifle for attending targets.

(Photos: Jack Appel).

Plate Numbers 160 & 161   New York State Military Model Remington Rolling Block, was given to Leon Backer in 1873 for attending targets.

(Photos: Jack Appel).

Another Remington rolling block military rifle, this one a Presentation Model, is shown on *Plate Numbers 162 and 163*. It is scroll and floral engraved with a different border around the action. The complete frame, trigger guard, hammer, breech block, tang and three sections of the barrel, butt plate, barrel bands, etc. are tastefully engraved. Has a nickel-plated band, gold-plated rear sight, etc. Inside the tangs on top is number 12957, on bottom tang is number 12957. This rifle too, is in .50-70 Gov't. caliber.

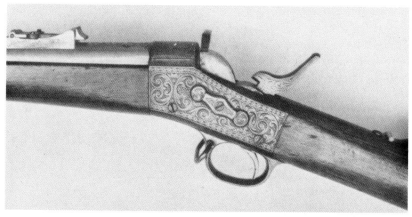

Plate Numbers 162 & 163   Remington Rolling Block Presentation Model in .50-70 caliber. (Photos: Jack Appel).

To continue the Remington story:—Next *Plate Number 164* shows a nicely engraved Remington Beals rifle. Several Beals specimens were shown in *Boys' Single Shot Rifles.* This specimen is engraved on the iron frame and on the rear of the barrel. It is serial numbered 679. Caliber is .32 rimfire. On top of the barrel it is marked: "Beals Patent, June 28, 1864—Jan. 30, 1866 E. Remington & Sons, Ilion, N. Y." On the top tang is engraved: "C. K. to J.L.B. 1871."

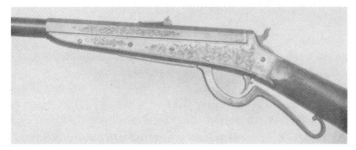

Plate Number 164   An Engraved Remington Beals—breech section. (Photo: Jack Appel).

A rifle which is quite rare and unusual in engraved form is the Number 4 Rolling Block which is on *Plate Number 165.* This little piece, the lightest rifle made on the Remington rolling block system, is serial numbered "50 307." It sports a 22½" part octagon, part round barrel in .22 rimfire caliber, marked on the top flat: "Remington Arms Co., Ilion N. Y." Action is completely scroll engraved, as is rear of the barrel flats. The buttstock and forend are both finely checkered. The forend has a hard rubber tip. All metal is silver plated. Overall length is 37".

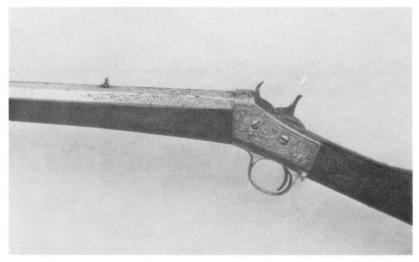

Plate Number 165   A specially engraved Model Number 4 Remington Rolling Rifle. (Photo: Jack Appel).

162

The Number 7 Remington is quite a scarce rifle, particularly scarce, and it may be more appropriate to call it quite rare in this form as illustrated on *Plate Number 166*. This is an offhand, or Scheutzen style, rifle on the rolling block Number 7 receiver. It has a 28½" light, part octagon, part round barrel in .22 Long Rifle caliber marked: "Remington Arms Co., Ilion, N. Y., U.S.A." Stocks are of imported walnut, checkered pistol grip and forearm, rubber pistol grip cap, Swiss, or Scheutzen, butt plate. It has a small Wind Gauge front sight and the special Lyman tang peep sight, usually furnished with this model. These were called "Target or Sporting Rifles." Serial number is 300 096. Overall length of rifle is 42½". This model was manufactured from 1903 to 1911.

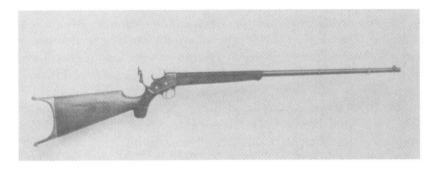

Plate Number 166   Remington Rolling Block Model 7 Offhand Rifle.

(Photo: Jack Appel).

A specially engraved Number 2 Remington rifle is shown on *Plate Numbers 167 and 168*. There is a small silver shield inlaid in the buttstock with initials, no doubt that of the original owner. The full octagon barrel is 28½" long. Rifle length overall is 45¼". The serial number, engraved on the lower tang is 39704. The caliber is .32-20 (32 WCF). This specimen has a beautiful pistol grip, cheekpiece stock with Scheutzen butt plate. Checkered grip and forend. The forend tip is silver plated, quite a beauty!

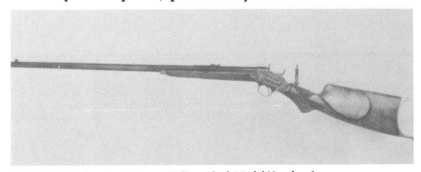

Plate Number 167   Remington Rolling Block Model Number 2.

(Photo: Jack Appel).

Plate Number 168   Close-up of action and engraving on rifle from Plate Number 167. (Photo: Jack Appel).

Animal engravings on Remingtons aren't common by any means. In fact, they are seldom seen. But look at *Plate Numbers 169 and 170* to see an early rolling block rifle with animals on one side and a pheasant and fox on the reverse. The animals are a doe lying down, and a wolf's head in a circular panel. This is an early .38 caliber rifle with a single set trigger, raising leaf peep sight, and the octagon barrel 26″ with octagon topped frame. Has the straight grip stock and metal tipped forend. The trigger guard, hammer, breech block and butt plate are all scroll engraved. The top tang is marked: "Remingtons, Ilion, N.Y., U.S.A." "Pat'd May 3, Nov. 16, 1864 Apr. 17." The number 2578 appears on the lower tang, stock, forend and butt plate, while the tangs are numbered inside 26383.

Plate Numbers 169 & 170   Close-up of animal engravings on action section of a Remington Rolling Block. (Photo: Jack Appel).

164

Another Military Pattern rifle, is a Brevette-Remington. *Plate Numbers 171 and 172* illustrates this grape and leaf decorated rifle. It has a 30″ damascus barrel .50-70 caliber. This barrel is inlaid in gold arabesque designs. The grape and leaf engraving appears on the frame, barrel, bands, trigger guard, forend tip and butt plate. The rear sight, of very unusual pattern, is an iron arch immediately in front of the receiver with two peep holes (for change in elevation). There is a 'loaded' indicator in the breech block. Serial number is 210 34.

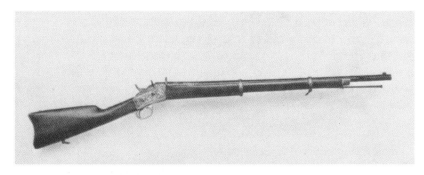

Plate Numbers 171 & 172   Engraved Brevette Remington Rolling Block Rifle, both sides breech section. (Photos: Jack Appel).

165

A foreign made rolling block which, while it is not a Remington fits in here. *Plate Number 173* illustrates a "Wafferfabrik-Steyr" engraved rolling block rifle, an interesting piece with a Norwegian type safety hammer. See *Volume One Single Shot Rifles*, for a discussion of this safety mechanism. The rifle has a 29″ octagon barrel with an open front sight and a military type folding leaf rear sight. It has a 'Monte Carlo' pattern stock of European walnut with cheekpiece, and it and the forend are nicely checkered. The rifle has the usual European swivels for a carrying strap and the forend is pinned to the barrel. The action frame, trigger guard, hammer, breech block and butt plate are all engraved with a scroll design. The words "Waffenfabrik-Steyr" are inlaid in gold on the barrel. There is also one gold band inlaid at rear of the barrel. The serial number is E1578.

Plate Number 173   Austrian-made "Waffenfabrik-Steyr" rolling block rifle.
Photo: Jack Appel).

Meanwhile, back to the Remington factory and the rolling block rifle displayed on *Plate Numbers 174 and 175*. This is a special Number One which is engraved and nickel-plated. Marked on the barrel "Pat. May 3, 1864, April 17, 1866." Serial number is 1773 and the caliber is marked on the underside of the barrel in the usual location, "44S." The stock of this rifle has two cheekpieces, one on each side. The stock also has two silver plate inlays. One on either side as shown in *Plate Numbers 176 and 177*. Quite a fine old rifle.

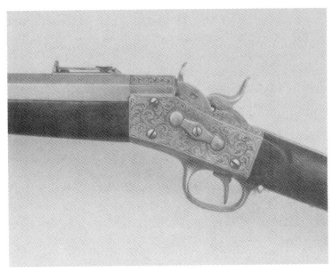

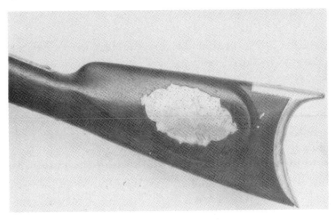

Plate Numbers 174, 175, 176 & 177 A Number One Model Remington Rolling Block Rifle, with fine engraving and two cheekpieces—one on each side of buttstock. (Photos: Jack Appel).

Next, we move into the Hepburn field of Remingtons. *Plate Number 178* shows a Hepburn which is in the rare caliber of .22 rimfire. Also unusual, is the cut down side walls and the altering of the breech block to seat a partially inserted .22 cartridge. This has a rather heavy full octagon barrel 30" long. Marked on the top of barrel "Remington Arms Co., Ilion, N.Y., U.S.A." The usual Hepburn markings appear on the left side of the receiver. It has a hooded front sight with removeable inserts and a Lyman 2A windage adjustable tang sight. The cut down sides of the action frame enable the fingers to insert or remove the cartridge easily. This rifle has the usual pistol grip Hepburn pattern stock and the plain forend and rifle butt plate of the last Hepburn series of the hi-power type. This is apparently a factory original rifle throughout. The bore is excellent and possibly a Walker rifled barrel. Serial numbers are 9991 and 9993.

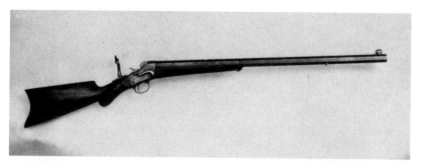

Plate Number 178   An unusual Remington-Hepburn. (Photo: Jack Appel).

Shown here are several of the rare Remington Walker under lever rifles. *Plate Numbers 179 and 180* show two views of a Walker Hepburn, the left side of the rifle with breech closed; and, the right side with the lever dropped and the action opened. This is serial number 3 of the Scheutzen Walker series—number W3 on the bottom tang and No. 3 on the face of the breech block. The frame is engraved on left side "Remington Scheutzen." Buttstock is marked "WHD" under the top tang and "00" under the bottom tang. The right tang is marked "00," and "6" on top and bottom. The butt plate is stamped "00." The rifle has a finely figured pistol grip, cheekpiece, Scheutzen buttstock and the scrolled trigger guard, which was standard on the Scheutzen model. (Please refer to page 129 and page 155 of *Single Shot Rifles*.)

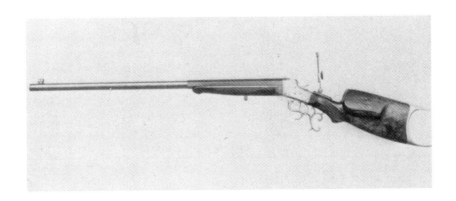

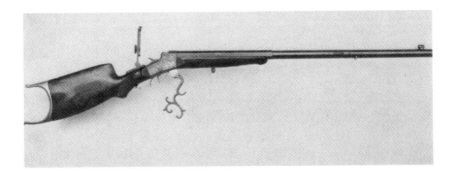

Plate Numbers 179 & 180   Remington Walker Scheutzen under lever rifle.

(Photos: Jack Appel).

Plate Numbers 181 and 182 illustrate a letter from the famous Dr. W. G. Hudson in which he mentions the new rifle (The Walker Under Lever Scheutzen) and also the Remington circular which announces the newest model.

169

DR. WALTER O. HUDSON
73 WEST 131ST STREET
NEW YORK CITY

TELEPHONE JOHN B. HARLEM

New York, APR 11 1904 190

Dear Mr. Thomas:

Yours of the 9th received. We of course investigated and found the cause of the mis-fire before sending you the cartridges. I once found the same defect in a 45/70 of the U.S. Ctg. Co's make, but that is the only previous time I ever found one.

Replying to your inquiries about Sea Girt, I am not very well posted on the subject, for since I left the N.J. I've never occupied a commission in Capt. & Asst. Surgeon in a New York regiment. The authorities at Sea Girt dont like me any more, but I can see that this is going to be the liveliest kind of a year for rifle shooting. *It is rumored that no Sea Girt team will come over.* In addition to the usual Sea Girt matches, there will be the National match at Fort Riley, Kansas; then there is the Bundesfest, the great German-American shooting festival, which occurs in June at Union Hill, N.J. Then there are the matches of the N.Y. State Rifle Assn., newly organized, which will take place at Creedmoor Sept. 17 to 17; this promises to have a larger attendance than the Sea Girt shoot. And Georgia and Ohio are also expected to run prize shoots. So you see the calendar will be full this year.

I enclose you a circular of a new rifle I have been helping the Remington Co. to develop, and a target made by Mr. Kelley with it. Having finished with that, I am working on some new ideas for further perfecting the 30 cal. bullet for long range shooting. I have not yet decided as to whether to develop these ideas through your company or through the Peters Ctg. Co., but think I am on the track of something good.

Yours sincerely,

W. O. Hudson

REMINGTON - SCHUETZEN
Match Rifle

NEW SPECIAL MODEL

 T H I S Rifle is made to meet the demand for a match rifle of most improved expert design of high-class workmanship, material and finish, and of extreme accuracy. It is nearer popular expert requirements than any Schuetzen rifle made in this country. The action is a modification of our No. 3 with under lever and sliding breech block so arranged as to force home a shell partially inserted in the chamber.

New design finger lever guard; fancy walnut stock with cheek piece, finely checkered, new improved and carefully adjusted hand-made double set triggers, special rear wind gauge Vernier sight and hood front sight with interchangeable pin head and aperture discs, specially designed Schuetzen Swiss butt plate, barrel 30 or 32 inch half octagon, weight from 11 to 13 pounds $60.00

Remington-Walker barrel, breech loading, extra	$12.00		
Palm rest, extra	5.00	$17.00	
Remington-Walker barrel, muzzle loading, with patent muzzle, starter, wooden rod, lubricator, sizer, bullet mould, etc., extra	$15.00		
Testing for guaranteed group within 2 1/4 inch circle at 200 yards . .	8.00	23.00	40.00
			$100.00

Price of parts furnished on application.

29

Plate Numbers 183 and 184 show another Remington Scheutzen. The first plate shows the full length rifle with both opened and closed breech and the second plate is a close-up of the action showing the engraved model name on the left side of the receiver. This fine rifle, a .38-55 caliber, has a 30 inch, full octagon barrel with a globe front sight and Remington vernier tang rear sight. The barrel is also milled for the Pope-type "claw" scope mounts. The action is, of course, the rare under lever Hepburn and has the 'typical production' straight grip, cheekpiece Scheutzen buttstock. The grip is checkered and the regular scrolled trigger guard covers double set triggers. The buttstock is marked "WHD" and "3" on all tangs and buttplate. The rifle is serial number 4. Marked on the lower tang is "N.W.4" and No. 4 on the face of the breech block. Length overall is 47½ inches and weighs 13 pounds. This rifle was at one time owned by H. A. Donaldson, as his name was engraved by him on the barrel under the forearm. This rifle was made by Remington for Dr. W. G. Hudson.

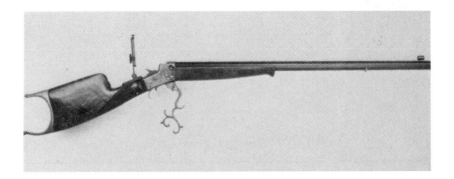

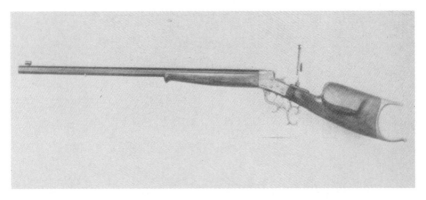

Plate Number 183   Remington Scheutzen made for Dr. W. G. Hudson.

(Photos: Jack Appel).

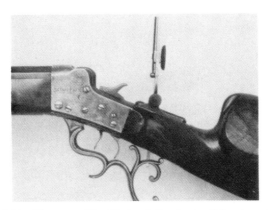

Plate Number 184   Close-up of Dr. Hudson's Remington Scheutzen rifle.
(Photo: Jack Appel).

The next rifle differs from the Scheutzen model under levers. *Plate Numbers 185 and 186* show one of the two known sporting rifles built on this particular system. It is a hunting grade rifle similar to the No. 3 High Power Hepburn in stock design and type of buttplate. (Refer to *Single Shot Rifles,* 129-130, 155, 162, 163).

The action is a regular under lever Hepburn with *pistol grip* and plain under lever. The tapered octagon barrel in .32-40 caliber is marked "Remington Arms Co., Ilion, N.Y., U.S.A." Serial number in the under lever series is No. 12 on the face of breech block, stock and butt plate, and the tangs. On the tangs under the wood is 1-9904. On the stock is "L. N. Walker." On the side of frame is "The Skinner, S. A. Medicus." There is quite a story concerning this rifle.

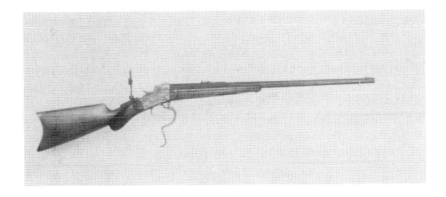

Plate Number 185   Remington Walker Sporting rifle—one of two known.
(Photo: Jack Appel).

173

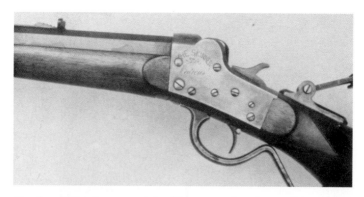

Plate Number 186   Close-up of the "Skinner-Medicus" Remington Walker Rifle. (Photo: Jack Appel).

The rifle was made for and owned by Doctor S. A. Skinner, a close friend and shooting companion of Dr. F. W. Mann, author of the authoratative *"The Bullets Flight from Powder to Target"* published in 1909. The word "Medicus" was Dr. Skinner's name for his woodchuck preserve near Hoosick Falls, New York, Dr. Skinner's hometown, (also possibly the doctor's nickname).

To quote Dr. Mann, page 88, "At this stage of rifle and ammunition experimenting, quite a voluminous correspondence was carried on with Dr. S. A. Skinner, of Hoosick Falls, N. Y., an old rifle crank and expert marksman. The writer has spent many companionable days at range and 'Medicus' woodchuck preserve." And again, from page 90, "Reference has been made a number of times to Dr. S. A. Skinner of Hoosick Falls, N. Y., and his sudden death, which occurred August 15, 1905, calls for a passing word. He was born in Thetford, Vt. Graduated from the university and was a general medical practitioner in his native state for 10 years, being appointed a medical examiner by Governor Holbrook, and assistant surgeon of the 7th Vermont Volunteer regiment. Owing to ill health, however, he was not allowed to take to the field with the regiment, and during 1864 moved with his family to Hoosick Falls, N. Y., where he resided the remainder of his life, one of the most prominent and successful physicians of Rensselaer County, and the leading practitioner of Hoosick Falls. He was an inventor of considerable note, including surgical instruments, a hospital bed, one of the first stethoscopes, the Skinner oiler, used on mowing machines, and many things of value and interest to the rifleman. He was a recognized authority and wrote quite extensively for *Shooting and Fishing*, under the nom de plume of 'Medicus' some of his best articles being published during the last few years of his life." Dr. Mann also shows a photo of Dr. Skinner along with himself and Major George Shockley taken at the Medicus Woodchuck Preserve.

Plate Number 187 shows the original L. N. Walker patent on the under lever.

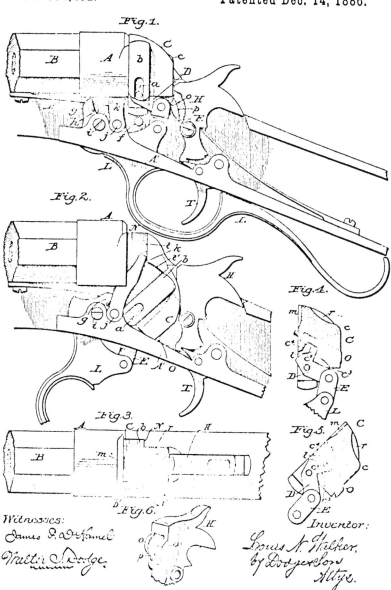

(No Model.)

L. N. WALKER.

BREECH LOADING GUN.

No. 354,452.

Patented Dec. 14, 1886.

Plate Number 187   The L. N. Walker Patent drawing.

Now, finally, one of the scarce Remington Number 5 Special High Power Rifles. This rifle, *Plate Number 188* is built on the special rolling block action. The 28″ round special smokeless steel barrel is chambered for the .30-40 cartridge. Marked on top of this barrel "Remington Arms Co., Ilion, N. Y., U.S.A." Marked on the bottom of the barrel ".30-40"; on the left side of the action frame is "Remington Arms Co., Ilion, N. Y., U.S.A." The serial number on bottom of tang is A. 181. Length overall is 43½″ and the weight is 7 lbs. This specimen has the automatic ejector. (They also came with a plain extractor and in 7 mm Mauser and other calibers as listed in *Single Shot Rifles.*

A few notes about the under lever Hepburn, or the L. W. Walker Patent and its variations which are interesting. Remington first catalogued the under lever rifle in their 1904-5 catalogue and then once again in 1909. The Remington Scheutzen is both illustrated and described in *"American Small Arms"* by E. S. Farrow, a book published in 1904. In *"Remington Firearms"* by Alden Hatch, the period of the manufacture of this rifle is given as 1904-1907; and, for the Hunters Rifle No. 3, the period of manufacture is mentioned as 1883-1907.

This particular Hunters Rifle has a two piece trigger guard with a small checkered spur projecting down from the rear of the trigger guard. This is to actuate the block by pushing it down and forward to open the block and, back and up to close it. This breech block is a straight up and down traveling block similar to that in the regular side lever operated Hepburn action. This rifle is illustrated in Hatch's book on Page 321. In an article in *The American Rifleman*, June 1935, titled "Rifles of Yesterday" by N. H. Roberts, the dates of manufacturing of the under lever Hepburn are given as 1902-05.

Mr. Roberts, being born in 1866, lived through the Scheutzen period, and died in 1948. His article illustrates a Remington Scheutzen with scroll under lever that was made for Dr. W. G. Hudson, serial number 4. This same rifle is shown on *Plates 183 and 184.* The letter from Dr. Hudson, also shown on *Plate 181* of this book mentions "I enclose you a circular of a new rifle I have been helping the Remington Company develop, and a target made by Mr. Walker with one of them. The circular *(Plate 182)* is of the Remington Scheutzen Special Model, just out." This circular is almost the same as the 1904-05 Remington catalogue page showing the rifle. Now to add more confusion about this, we have noted the mention in Dr. F. W. Mann's book *"The Bullet's Flight"*, the fact his friend, Dr. Skinner, who died on August 15, 1905, also owned an under lever Hunting or Sporting pattern Hepburn. *(Also shown in this chapter on Plates 185 and 186).*

The original L. N. Walker Patent Number 354,452 was a Hepburn patent 'Improvement' coming 7 years after the original L. L. Hepburn Patent of Oct. 7, 1879. This Walker patent number 354,452 is described as pertaining to "an action with under lever and sliding breech block so arranged as to force home a shell partially inserted in the chamber."

The only rifle with this feature, as described in the Walker Patent document, is described and illustrated in *More Single Shot Rifles* on page 99 and 100. The breech block of this rifle is marked "L. W. Walker Patent."

Now there are several puzzling and confusing aspects about these dates. How could Farrow's book, published in 1904, have the Remington-Scheutzen Walker photo and description the same year as Dr. Hudson's letter said "the new model just introduced?" To resolve this perhaps someone should jump to the conclusion that Dr. Hudson was late in mentioning the model (possibly he just learned of it); and too, Remington probably released the data and photo of it to Mr. Farrow earlier. It must have been earlier, as it takes time to get a book on the market; and, it could have been in Farrow's hands as early as 1902 or 1903.

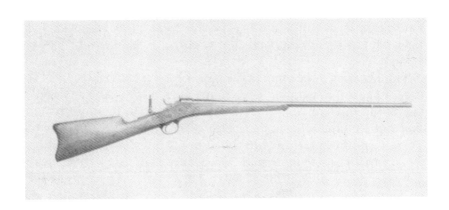

Plate Number 188   Remington Number 5 Special High Power Rifle.
(Photo: Jack Appel).

XI

The Single Shot as a Foundation

In the past I have shown various remodeled single shots in which the old actions were used to build usable rifles in various calibers. I have never been guilty of using the actions of a fine original rifle to rebarrel, restock or otherwise alter to obtain a new rifle in a modern caliber.

This has been done often in the past, I have mentioned some of the times I knew it to happen. Even in the days of the 1920's and 1930's, before the fine old rifles were much appreciated, there were many shot out or otherwise undesirable, plain models floating around. These could be obtained cheaply, even for those days, I remember, when I first became interested. Winchester high side wall actions or old rifles could be had for $5.00 to $10.00 each. The Stevens 44½ pieces were about the same prices. The set trigger Winchester and Stevens ran a little more, generally $9.00 to $12.50 for a decent action. Engraved Stevens 44½ actions, engraved Ballard No. 6 and 6½ actions usually brought about $35.00 then, and that was considered high. Many times fine engraved Stevens and Ballard complete rifles in very good or better shape could be had for the same prices.

So, there was never any real excuse for tearing up a good rifle to get an action to build a .22 Hornet or a .22-3000 R2 Lovell cartridge varmint rifle. Through the years I have had many rifles made for various new cartridges as they appeared on the market. I also had quite a few wildcats made as well as some experimental calibers. These have all been made by using old actions I had on hand, most of which had been in my possession for years, from the days when they were cheap and plentiful.

Even with an action which was on hand and available, (at an old low price), the cost of barreling and stocking these became increasingly more expensive. It has reached the point in the past few years where it has become prohibitive.

More and more reproduction and new single shot actions and rifles have become available the past few years; to the point it is more reasonable and much quicker to buy a Ruger Number One or a Browning Model 78 which are still lower in price, and thus acquire a good reproduction in any modern caliber you might require.

To buy an old single shot action, have it remodeled to suit, rebarreled, restocked, reblued, etc., entails a much larger investment in view of the high price the old actions will bring today. Some, like myself, would still do it this way, of course, since we prefer the original actions. However, I haven't had any new ones made up for several years and am not likely to do so, since I am out of actions and I have found the remodeled pieces will not command enough price to break even on the cost involved. Most people seem to prefer buying an old action only and thus create their own versions.

Many of these pieces I have had built in the past are gone now. They were used mainly for experimental shooting, almost none were shot at game or at varmints. I always had more varmint rifles than there were actual varmints in my home county, so the rifles were mainly shot at paper targets to determine just what accuracy they were capable of.

At any rate, I wish to show you some of these rifles, not to brag about their number or to hold them up as models of excellence in design, but principally, to show you just how involved it is possible to become when you are a single shot nut.

Many of these remodeled rifles have exotic woods used in the stocks. This is because, while I like American and European walnuts very much I had at one time a very large collection of American and foreign single shot rifles, practically all of which had in the higher grades, beautiful American, English, French, Italian and Circassian walnuts used in them by the various manufacturers of the era from the 1860's into the early years of this century, when these rifles were made.

Some exotic woods are suitable for gun stocks, some are not, but most are interesting and different. There are several more varieties I can think of now, I would liked to have tried, but time simply did not permit.

Plate Number 189 illustrates three rifles. From the top: This rifle is built on the Australian Cadet or training rifle action. These are, or were, plentiful and when the .310 original rifle was obtained, were selling for about $12.00 to $15.00 each. This rifle was fitted with a new .22 Hornet barrel by the late Charles C. Johnson and he also bushed the firing pin, installed a large knurled head takedown screw and drilled the back wall of the frame so the lower tang-block-lever assembly could be removed and the rifle cleaned from the breech. (This has always been the only objection I had to the Peabody-Martini. I was not able to clean the guns from the rear.) The stocks were semi-inletted, semi-finished pecan wood obtained from Reinhart Fajen and attached by me. It shot very well, as most good Hornet rifles do, and is still not obsolete for a settled countryside such as mine.

The second rifle, on *Plate Number 189*, is an experimental job. I had this old 44½ Stevens double set trigger action for a long time, and had Johnson fit one barrel for the .256 Winchester Magnum cartridge and the second barrel for a .22 Remington Jet cartridge. Both take the same size extractor since the heads of both cartridges are the same size. We made it takedown using the excellent Stevens system, and I wanted to learn if these revolver cartridges would shoot well in a rifle barrel. They did. . . .so that was accomplished, and the piece passed on. The stocks were obtained in semi-inletted form from Fajen's and were of quilted hard maple. I put them on the rifle and had them checkered professionally. The lever had been altered before I obtained this action. It was from a Stevens Scheutzen rifle, cut off and brazed onto the plain front end. It was sufficient, but the brazing didn't blue, of course. I found the brass oxidizing or blackening made by Birchwood Casey colored it well enough to match the balance of the lever.

The last rifle on this plate is a Winchester Low Wall action with an early breech block. This was rebarreled to the .17 caliber using the .218 Bee case. This was an experimental rifle and was soon passed on, when I learned there were better cases to use for a .17 caliber rifle. These stocks were also from Fajen and were made of persimmon, a very dense and hard wood, but not too handsome, as it had little, if any, figure. Forend tip and grip cap are South American, (possibly Brazilian) rosewood.

180

Plate Number 189 Remodeled Single Shots from author's collection.

Plate Number 190 shows three more custom single shots. Top is a Stevens 404-44½ rifle which was relined years ago by Charles C. Johnson, and which came to me in that state. The liner is chambered for the .22-3000 R2, commonly called the Lovell. This, of course, after Hervey Lovell, the late Indianapolis riflesmith. He developed the original .22-3000 Lovell cartridge using the .25-20 single shot case, necking it down to .22 caliber. The .22-3000 R2 was an improvement upon Lovell's cartridge and refers to the second version offered by Risley, another gunsmith and experimenter. This cartridge became very popular, before the advent of the .22 Hornet. It remained popular for years, and still is with those of us who still have some usable brass. This rifle has stocks of curly maple.

The rifle in the center is a Ballard I had made when the Remington 5 mm rimfire cartridge came on the market. I wished to try this new rimfire hot shot cartridge but did not care for the only rifle made for it, the Remington bolt action job. I had an old Ballard No. 2 action which was somewhat pitted on the frame, but cleaned it up and a friend engraved it with a scroll design to camoflauge the roughness of the outside. Bill Van Horne then made a nice, light weight, tapered octagon barrel in .20 caliber, fitted it to the action and chambered it for the new 5 mm Remington cartridge. We thought it best to use the one piece Ballard extractor instead of the two piece type as was used by Marlin on their .22 Ballard rifles. Since Remington had some problems with this hot one, they went to special extractor systems on their bolt action made in this caliber. Van Horne made an extractor, the extracting tip of which was inletted very shallowly into the rear of the chamber and it worked fine. This is a hot number in the cartridge line and was Remington's attempt to meet the Winchester Rimfire Magnum. It is now discontinued or, at least the Remington rifle for this cartridge has been discontinued. I have always felt if they had used a shortened, (and necked to .20 caliber), .22 Hornet case so it could have been reloaded, it would have been much better, and certainly cheaper to shoot.

This 5 mm Ballard rifle has screw-bean mesquite stocks on it. These semi-inletted blanks were obtained from Reinhart Fajen. The wood is rather scarce in sizes capable of use for stocking purposes, and is quite dense and hard. It is marked very strikingly, but not really handsome. It is unusual and turned out to be an interesting rifle.

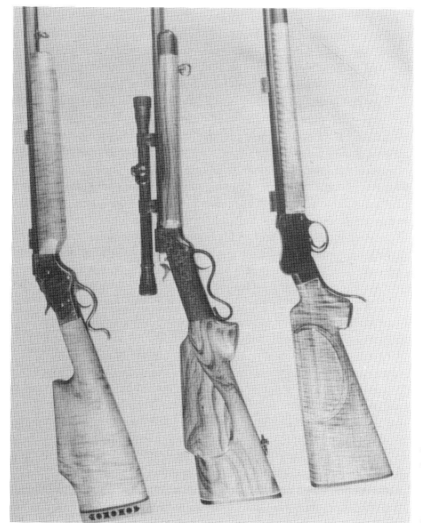

The last rifle on *Plate Number 190* is another Aussie Cadet action which was barreled for the .22 Jet pistol cartridge. It was stocked in curly maple and the finger lever altered to lie under the hand over the pistol grip. After experimenting with the standard Jet, which delivered much more velocity than that obtained in the revolvers chambered for it, Johnson rechambered this barrel for the magnum Jet, (called by various names). This turned out to be a very short necked, sharp shouldered case and the factory Jet cases didn't stand it too well. However, I found that by using new .357 Magnum brass, necking it down, then annealing the necks and shoulders, it would stand the expansion and be capable of reloading several times. Some extreme velocities (and pressures too) were had with this one but it went the way of most and was passed on to another owner.

Plate Number 191 contains three more experimental rifles, the first of which, is a Stevens 44½—47 double set trigger rifle. It was rebarreled by Parker Ackley to the .17 caliber cartridge which was introduced and used for a while by Harrington & Richardson in their .17 caliber high power rifle. The case used in this rifle was the .223. The stocks on this rifle were very beautifully figured crotch butternut. It is unusual to be able to get this wood. I only managed because I found a dealer who had cut it, dried it carefully and saved it to use himself one day. This wood is, of course, very similar to walnut, being of the same family, usually called 'white walnut.' Sometimes it is a much softer wood than regular black walnut but in this instance since it was from the crotch it was much harder and more dense. It made a very beautiful and unusual rifle. I found the large case .17 caliber to be more "boiler room" than I liked so it passed out of my hands, as most have.

The rifle in the center is one of the several made to test the .22 Extra Long Centerfire cartridge. This is the old .22 C.F. Stevens and Maynard. This rifle is built on a first model Stevens 44 double set trigger action. The light full octagon barrel was made to my specifications by Bill Van Horne with .228 groove diameter. I have tried many loads in this one and finally got it shooting into 1½ inches at 100 yards after getting the right bullet for it. The standard bullet for this cartridge was the .228 45 grain, but I have been unable to make it shoot as I thought it should, even in a perfect barrel on a Maynard Number 15 rifle. That rifle was shown in *Volume One Single Shot Rifles*.

This Stevens will shoot using the Lyman #225107 and the longer #225438 lead bullets. The load that performed the best is: 4.3 Gr. #80 powder. Another very accurate load was 3.2 and 3.5 grains of Dupont Marksman, a powder which has been discontinued. The wood used on this piece is honey locust, which is quite hard and

Plate Number 191   Experimental Single Shot Rifles.

possesses a grain which has the general appearance of oak. The wood has some reddish streaks here and there which makes it a little more interesting than an oak stock would be. The vermillion pistol grip cap and forend tip were added by me to these Fajen roughed-out stocks.

The last rifle on this plate illustrates my first attempt to get a .22 Extra Long Centerfire cartridge to shoot. This is an 044½ Stevens which I had rebarreled by Charles C. Johnson back in the early 1930's. We used a .22 caliber rimfire barrel from Stevens and Charley chambered it; as he had then, a reamer he had made to do some work on a 5.5 mm Velo Dog. This barrel was tight since it was made for the .22 caliber rimfire cartridge and was no improvement. All later barrels used were .228 which was the way Maynard and Stevens bored them. The rifle was used with the full length Stevens telescopic sight which came on the original rifle barrel, a .22-15-60 caliber.

Plate Number 192 also shows three rifles. Top is a Winchester Low Wall action which came with the steel shotgun buttstock shown. Harold Armstrong had made up a little .410 bore shotgun for his grandson and when I saw it, talked him into making another. The smooth bored barrel came from a Pennsylvania barrel works and Harold fitted the barrel with two screw-on, or off, chokes for the muzzle. He also made a new forend tipped with a piece of curly maple. I have only shot the gun at skeet, and, of course, doubles must of necessity be taken one at a time, since I found it impossible, (for me at least), to reload fast enough to shoot the doubles in the regular manner.

The center rifle is a Stevens Favorite which had one of the original Stevens-made Favorite barrels, (they were sold by a large parts company in the East years ago), put on in place of the ruined original barrel. The wood was beyond redemption so a new stock and a Mannlicher-style forend were fitted to the old action and the new barrel. It's just a nice little squirrel rifle.

The bottom piece is a Sharps Borchardt sporting rifle with an octagon barrel and an octagon topped receiver ring. These octagon top receivers seem to be rather scarce. It is generally seen on the Borchardt Express Rifle for the .45—2 7/8" Sharps case. The caliber of this particular rifle is .45 2.1" which is, of course, the same case as the later .45-70. Just a plain hunting or sporting rifle with the unusual frame.

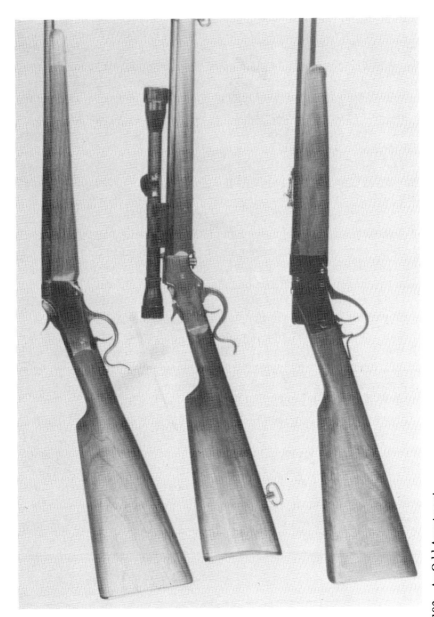

Plate Number 193 shows from the top, a Winchester Hi Wall action with the Winchester double Scheutzen set triggers and a plain finger lever. This rifle was made for me by John McPheeters when the .225 Winchester cartridge was introduced, using a Douglas barrel.

I again wanted unusual wood so managed to talk Reinhart Fajen into restocking this one in zebra wood, an extremely hard and dense wood. This species, from Africa, is generally used only for revolver and pistol grips or forend tips, pistol grip caps, etc. An excellent cartridge; of course, no better than the Improved Zipper we used for years, but easier to obtain since it is a factory loaded number and we always were forced to "roll our own" with any of the Zipper versions, which were all wild cats.

The center rifle is a double set Remington Hepburn which was only an action when it came to me. Rebarreled by Ackley for the .17 Hornet case, it was restocked along the pattern used on the Mid- and Long-Range Hepburn target rifles. A very fine little cartridge, that .17 Hornet, and ample noise and reach for a settled country such as we have here. It always used Lee 17, 18 and 20 grain bullets as I felt that weight was more in keeping with the small capacity of this case than the 25 grain .17 caliber bullets used in most rifles of .17 bore.

The bottom rifle on this plate is a Stevens 44½ double action with a .20 caliber barrel made in Oregon and fitted by Charley Johnson. It was chambered for the .20 caliber based upon the necked-down Hornet brass. Again, most .20 calibers used much larger cases, such as .222 Remington .223, etc. I wanted to use light bullets in this to be in balance with a small case and experimented with 27, 33 and 38 grain bullets which I obtained from a maker in California.

Frank Hempsted of Sunland, California, now deceased, furnished the chambering reamer used in this barrel. Frank did much experimenting with the .20 caliber but he preferred the larger cases. This rifle shot well for me. The stocks were on this action when I obtained it, though the forend piece had to be bushed down to fit the new barrel. It had a very heavy .22 rimfire barrel, of unknown origin, mounted when I obtained it, mainly for the double set action.

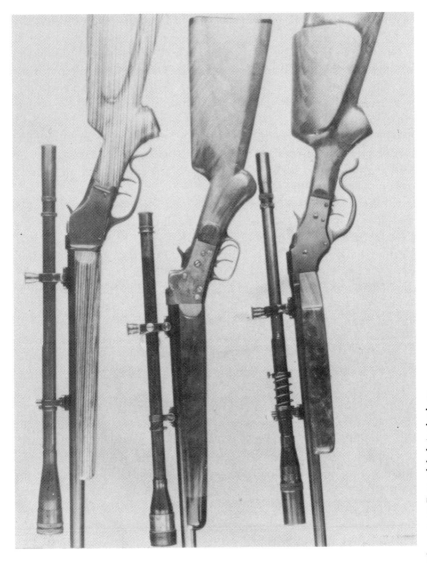

Plate Number 194 presents three more remodeled pieces. First, at the top is a Sharps-Borchardt which had double set triggers made to order by John McPheeters. He also installed a wing type safety which comes out on the left side of the frame through one of the existing large screw filled holes. John installed the Douglas barrel in .225 Winchester caliber and Harold Armstrong made the stocks from fine European walnut, which I had obtained from Flaig's in Pittsburgh, Pa.

The rifle in the center of the plate is a Winchester high side wall, takedown in the .225 Winchester caliber. The lever was altered from the plain, double Scheutzen set type to an under-the-band version, by a friend. Barreled by Charles C. Johnson who also did the action work to handle the rimless case and also bushed the block and installed the Mann-Niedner firing pin. The wood used, which doesn't photograph well, is Pacific Madrone, a west coast variety of hard maple. It is a well figured burly blank quite hard, of course, and of a pleasing pinkish-tan color.

The lower rifle is a Holland & Holland Farquharson which was originally in 8 x 57 JR caliber. Parker Ackley installed a barrel of his manufacture and chambered it for his 6 mm Short Krag. I had wanted it made in a .243 Winchester but Parker objected to this caliber because of the quite slanted firing pin used in this system and also because of the difficulty in milling for a good extractor to handle the rimless case. So, we used the .30-40 Krag case necked to the 6 mm caliber and shortened somewhat. This rifle was superbly accurate with the 70 grain 6 mm bullets at 100 yards, the longest distance at which I targeted the rifle while I owned it. The stocks are made of well marked French walnut, a blank I had picked up some years before at a gun show.

Three more converted rifles will be found on *Plate Number 195*. The top rifle another experimental piece made for a pistol cartridge. This is a Winchester high side wall single shot which was quite rough. After being engraved in a simple floral pattern, the rough pitted frame looked about 1000 percent bette: . Charles C. Johnson installed a barrel and chambered it for the .221 Remington "Fireball" pistol number. I wanted to see how it shot in a rifle and was told if it did not work well, it would be a simple matter to run a .222 reamer in and deepen this chamber. The .221 and .222 Remington cases are exactly the same at the rear, however, it shot very well so was never altered. E. C. Bishop & Sons made and installed the American walnut stocks and checkered them well.

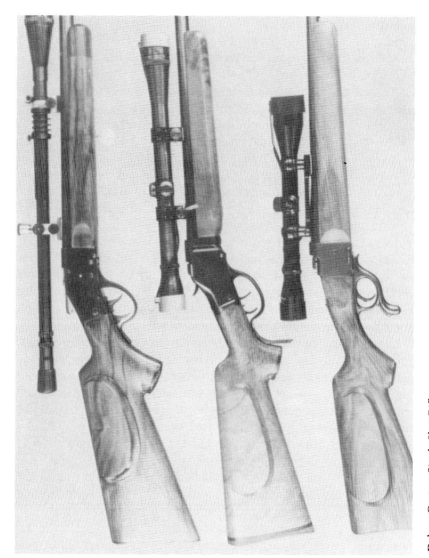

The middle rifle on this plate is another Winchester high side wall takedown action with a Douglas barrel installed by Charles C. Johnson and chambered for the .222 Remington Magnum cartridge. The tangs of this action frame had both been brazed to repair them, so I decided to see what could be done with a "through bolt" system. I shortened both tangs, had a local man weld a threaded block onto the underside of the upper tang to take a long bolt. He also altered the finger lever. I then tried my hand at making the stocks, fitting them to the altered tangs using the stock bolt. I also used a wood screw through the bottom end of the lower tang after it was bent to suit, this to hold fast the tang to the wood.

It turned out rather well since it was all new work for me. I am certainly not a stock maker, and it took me forever to get it done; but, it fits well and is quite solidly attached to the frame.

The lower rifle on this plate is one made up by Jerry Gebby when he was located in Dayton, Ohio. In this one Mr. Gebby, who is well known for his .22 Varminter made on the 250-3000 case, lined the original part octagon Winchester barrel for the .22-3000 cartridge. The chamber used is somewhat different from the R2 version, being a shorter necked, sharper shoulder variety. The rifle was not made for me as I acquired it after it was relined, so I am not sure just what this cartridge version was called. I fire formed regular R2 G & H cases in it and it shot well, as all Lovell calibers have for me. The case would accept a trifle more 4227 or 4198 powder than the regular R2 so, I assume it was delivering more velocity with the 41 grain Sisk bullets I was using at that time.

Look at *Plate Number 196* to observe more remodeled single shot action rifles. The top rifle is built on one of the Winchester high side wall, thick wall takedown actions found by James Serven shortly after World War Two at the Winchester factory. These actions were incomplete and there were no parts left there to complete them. The frames were new and unused and had been proof marked with the WP mark, and blued. I finally found the parts to complete it and Charles Johnson altered a flat spring hammer to operate correctly in this take down coil spring action. It laid around for years until the .444 Marlin cartridge was introduced, and for lack of something more interesting, it was barreled for that cartridge. I had found a fine piece of Circassian walnut and my friend, Armstrong, made the stocks using a steel Niedner type grip cap, a steel trap butt plate with provision for three .444 cartridges in the buttstock and a forend tip of Indian Buffalo horn. I found after shooting it that it was quite accurate at 100 yards using cast .44 caliber pistol bullets delivering 1¾ to 2½" groups. I also fired some factory jacketed bullet loads

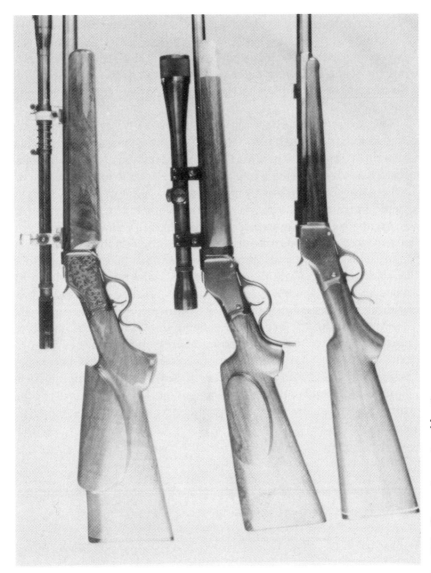

Plate Number 195   Conversions using old actions.

with somewhat better results. I obtained some newer, heavier jacketed bullets for this cartridge but did not get around to trying them out. It was a fine rifle and I thought would have made a good short range deer or bear rifle.

In the center of this plate is a Sharps-Borchardt military action with a Charles C. Johnson-fitted Douglas barrel for the .222 rimmed case. This is the Australian-made brass which was developed in Victoria for use in the Martini Cadet actions popular and plentiful "Down Under." This avoided the irksome job of making an extractor to handle the regular rimless case of the .222. The wood is an interesting piece of Oregon myrtle. It does not show in this photo, but the wood is of light color with dark streaks throughout. Forend tip and grip cap are Fajen's Brazilian rosewood. It shoots extremely well.

The lower rifle on this illustration is built on a Winchester high side wall action which came to me with the lower tang and the lever altered to the form shown. The upper tang was also bent upward almost at right angles when I got the frame. I have no idea who altered the tang in this manner, nor do I know what a previous owner had in mind when he bent these parts. It was different from any conversions (or perversions) I have seen. I thought this was my chance to make a thumb-hole stock for a single shot rifle. I have seen many bolt actions and shotguns with thumb-hole stocks on them. Harold Armstrong said "Let's make one," which he did, using a nice piece of French walnut, and Johnson installed the barrel, block bushing and extractor for the .222 Remington rimless cartridge. It fit me very well, partly because the friend who did the stocking job was also a southpaw shooter. Charley chambered it for the WRA Co. .222 brass and it handled this most excellently. It would not shoot or extract as well with Remington brass. There is apparently just enough difference in the two makes of brass to cause a minor difference when the chamber is made to minimum tolerance as it should be.

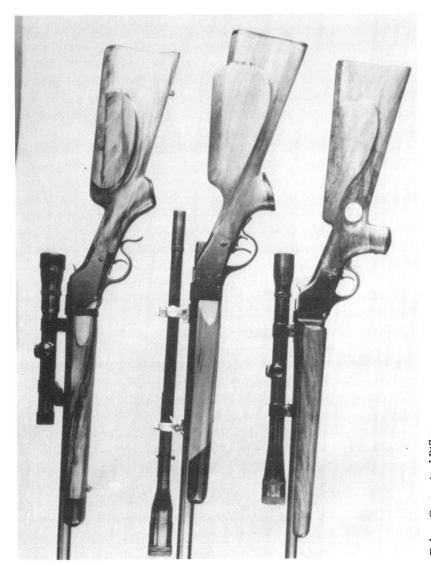

Plate Number 196   More Deluxe Customized Rifles.

195

Plate Number 197 shows four rifles. The top rifle is a Griffin & Howe Winchester high side wall, thick wall frame with the lever beautifully contoured for under-the-hand use, also by G. & H. These actions were obtained by G. & H. back in the 1930's and barreled for the .22 Hornet, .22 rimfire and .22-3000 R2 cartridges. These were advertised in the *American Rifleman* magazine in the 1930's and were deluxe rifles in every respect with well-figured walnut stocks, horn tipped forestock, etc. My specimen was made in .22-3000 R2 caliber and was so marked. It had been rechambered for the .219 Wasp cartridge sometime during or shortly after World War Two and that is the way I shot it. Cases were difficult to make so, it was passed on to another who wanted a Wasp.

The second rifle from the top on *Plate Number 197* is the J. E. Gebby reline job in .22-3000 Max Lovell previously described.

Third from the top is a Winchester low side wall rifle with an A. O. Niedner, Dowagiac, Michigan, barrel for the .22 Hornet cartridge. The stocks on the rifle were made of quite curly cherry finished in a dark tone.

The bottom rifle is a .14 caliber rifle made by Alton "14 Caliber" Jones of Portland, Oregon. Mr. Jones did a lot of pioneering work on .14 and .17 caliber cartridges back in the 1930's. I became acquainted with Alton after *Volume Three Boys Single Shot Rifles* was published. He wrote, saying he had had one of the Number Fifteen Hamilton rifles when he was a boy and would like to own one again. I found a good specimen for $15.00 about 1969 and sent it to him. He was much elated and so presented me with the little .14 caliber rifle shown. This has a Winchester low side wall action with a Springfield .30-06 barrel lined by Jones to .14 caliber. He had made just a very few of these, and in addition, made one or two solid barrels bored and rifled in .14 caliber. This rifle is chambered for the 5.5 mm Velo Dog case necked to .14 caliber. He sent me formed cases, also new unformed 5.5 cases, forming and necking dies, and a bullet mould for a 16 grain .14 caliber grooved bullet. This mould had two .14 caliber cavities as well as the original Ideal cavity for a .22 caliber bullet. He merely turned the mould over and after cherrying out the cavities made a new cut off plate and fastened it in place on the side opposite the original cut-off. He had also made a mould for a gas check .14 caliber bullet but this was accidently ruined when he was making another cavity in the mould for a different caliber.

I did get very few of the gas check bullets made by the original cavity; however, he made dies and formed jacketed .14 caliber soft nose bullets for use in this and other .14 caliber rifles. He stated the jacketed bullets ahead of 4 ½ grains of Hercules 2400 had accounted for several coyotes in his native Oregon. He had at one time used the .22 Hornet case as a basis for his .14's but said it was not as satisfactory as the 5.5 mm Velo Dog brass even though it was much easier to get the Hornet brass.

I have used this little .14 caliber rifle on squirrel and the 16 grain lead bullet does a good job when only head shots are taken. My favorite load with this is: 2.3 to 2.6 grains Green Dot. I have also used loads of 2.2 gr. to 2.4 grains of Dupont Marksman's powder. This powder was apparently discontinued in the late 1920's or very early 1930's. I never saw it listed for sale anywhere, but bought an old Dupont can partially full about 1974. Alton also made some .17 caliber rifles and was playing with these as well as the .14's before everyone else got into the act, actually back in the 1920's.

I have one of his .17 Hornet rifles also on a low wall action with a solid steel barrel of his manufacture. He was playing with a .17 Hornet barrel which he called 'Scorpion' and it was on a Stevens 44½ action. This barrel was experimental, with a much quicker twist. His Hornet cases were necked to .17 caliber, the original head stamping removed and restamped with "A.J. .17." He told me he, too, preferred the smaller cases for his experimental calibers and always felt it wasn't necessary to "light up a super market with large amounts of powder."

Jones had made dies to draw and form the .14 caliber jacketed bullets, and though I did get samples of these bullets and samples of the different draws used in fabrication of the bullets, I did not obtain these dies. They were made by Jones for use on a large heavy press he owned and he passed away before I could learn what the press was or could obtain these dies. So the passing of my friend left many questions unanswered. He was an extremely talented and interesting person.

Plate Number 198 displays a single rifle, an experimental job in .22 Extra Long Centerfire. This one is on a Winchester low side wall action with a single set trigger. The barrel used was a new Remington .22 Long Rifle caliber and was enlarged in the bore and also in the grooves, the latter being .228. Ward Koozer was still working at that time and did a fine job on this work. Charles Johnson fitted and chambered the barrel. The stocks were made and installed by Fajen's and are of American lacewood, which is our old friend sycamore with a new, more attractive name. It has zebra wood trim. This rifle shot extremely well, but only with small

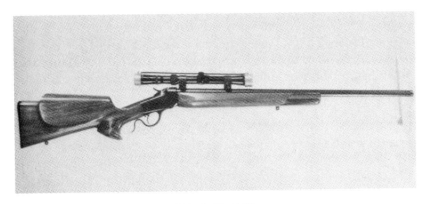

Plate Number 198   Experimental Single Shot Rifle.

charges of DuPont Bulk Shotgun Smokeless. I had a small supply of this left, formerly using it for priming charges in Scheutzen rifles when I shot those years ago. I always sieved the powder into two or three sizes of grains and used the fine granulations for priming and for these small cartridges as a full charge. It is very good for this use, but of course, has been discontinued for many years. I tried DuPont 4227, 1204, 4198, Hercules 2400, Red Dot, Green Dot, BLC from Hodgdon's and Reloader #7, but nothing worked as well.

I finally decided after playing with six or seven rifles in the .22 Ex. L.C.F. caliber, that the cartridge was never capable of really fine accuracy; and, could not be compared with that obtained with the .22 Long Rifle in a good match barrel. If I could only get some of that fine grained powder Remington used in their 5 mm rimfire . . .

Plate Number 199 illustrates the .14 caliber mould made by Alton Jones for the rifle shown on *Plate 172.*

(Since we are on the subject of moulds, you notice I use the old form of the word, spelling it with a "u." This is to differentiate from the "mold" which is commonly found on such cheeses as Roquefort, Stilton, etc.)

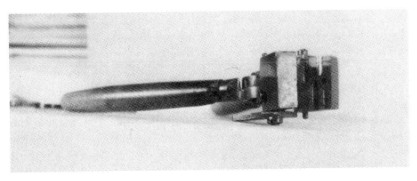

Plate Number 199   The Alton Jones .14 Caliber mould.

Plate Number 200 shows an unusual mould. This one is also marked 'Ideal.' This, I believe to be a mould for casting keel weights for use on wooden duck and goose decoys. I don't find this mould shown in any of the old **Ideal Handbooks,** but I feel sure it was made by this company.

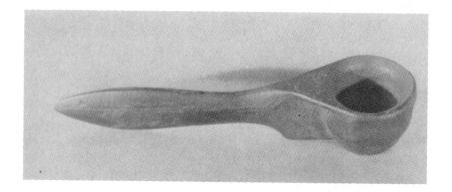

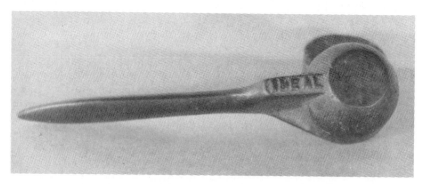

Plate Number 200   An Ideal decoy weight "mould".

In the *Ideal Handbook Number 25* there is illustrated on a full page, an advertisement of the Marlin Firearms Company for the Marlin Decoy Body Weight at $1.50 per dozen. This is a semi-hemispherical lead weight with a wooden screw cast into it for attaching to the bottom of the decoy. In this same issue of the Handbook are several other full page ads by Marlin as well as those of other firearms companies. This was common practice when these early Handbooks were current. (Incidentally, this same issue of the *Ideal Handbook* carried the announcement by John H. Barlow of the sale of the Ideal Manufacturing Company to The Marlin Firearms Company, who operated it for some time, later selling it to the Lyman Gun Sight Corporation.)

Plate Number 201

Plate Number 201 is: "Alton Jones Cartridge & Jacketed Bullet Draws." Shown left to right.
1. Velo Dog 5.5 mm cartridge box. Leaning against this box is a Jones copper disc which is used to form the bullet jacket draws.
2. .14 caliber Jones cartridge based on the Velo Dog case.
3. Five draws to form .14 caliber jacketed bullets.
4. Two finished jacketed bullets, .14 caliber.
5. The lead core for jacketed bullets.

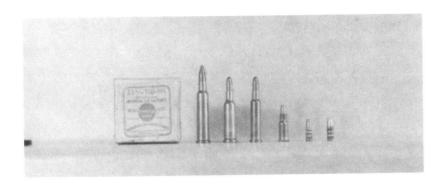

Plate Number 202

Plate Number 202: "Alton Jones .17 and .14 Caliber Cartridges." Shown left to right.
1. A Velo Dog cartridge box.
2. Alton Jones .17 Hornet cartridge.
3. Alton Jones .14 Hornet cartridge.
4. Alton Jones .14 caliber cartridge on the Velo Dog case.
5. Alton Jones .14 caliber cartridge on the .22 Long Rifle case.
6. Alton Jones .14 caliber lead bullets with gas checks.

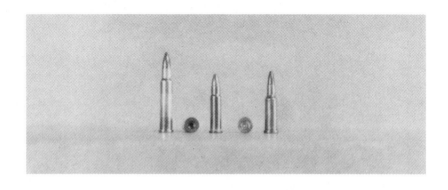

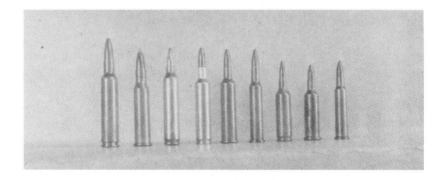

Plate Number 203

Plate Number 203 illustrates several .17, .20 and .22 caliber cartridges. At the top of the plate are .17 and .20 caliber and on the lower part of this photo are the .17 and .22 calibers. Shown left to right—(top part of plate).

1. .20 caliber cartridge on .22 Hornet case.
2. The head of an Alton Jones .17 Hornet case, head stamped: AJ .17
3. The Remington 5 mm (.20 caliber) Rimfire Magnum cartridge.
4. The head of the .17 Hornet Hummingbird cartridge.
5. The Frank Hempsted .17 Hummingbird cartridge.
   Left to right—(bottom of plate).
1. Weatherby .224 Magnum cartridge.
2. Australian .222 rimmed .22 caliber case.
3. Harrington & Richardson .17 caliber cartridge.
4. .222 Remington .17 caliber cartridge (nickel case).
5. Australian .222 rimmed case necked to .17 caliber.
6. .22-3000 R2 on Griffin & Howe case.
7. .17 caliber cartridge on Remington .221 "Fireball" case.
8. Ackley .17 Bee cartridge.
9. Alton Jones .17 caliber cartridge on the .22 Hornet case.

202

INDEX

INDEX

Italics Indicates Illustrations

BROWNING, Val. 144
B.S.A. (rear sight), 13, 21.
BULLARD, 69.
BULL FROG SR., 45.

C

CAIN, Jim, 6.
CHAPMAN, Wm., 118.
CLARK, Roe S., Jr., 12.
CLIVE, A.A., *25*, 26, 27, 28, 29, 30.
CLOW, Milton, 90.
    (Collection, 90)
COLEMAN, Chas. C., 68.
CONGRESS, U.S., 14.
CRAWFORD, Dr. John, 100, 101.
CROZIER, Jerry, 69.
CUTTER, C.N., 98.

D

DANGERFIELD, F. S. & COMPANY, 72, 73, 74.
DANGERFIELD & LEFEVER, 72, 73.
DICKERMAN, A., 76.
DICKSON, JOHN & SON, 77.
DONALDSON, H.A., 171
D.P. COMPANY, 3.

E

EGDORF, Harry, 107, *108*.
ELLIS, J.A., 72.
EMPIRE STATE CADET RIFLE, 35, 36, *37*.
E. REMINGTON & SONS, 68, 74, 88, 154, 161.

F

FAJEN, RINEHART, 179, 181, 185, 187, 193, 197.
FARROW ARMS COMPANY, 86
       (Standard Grade Target Rifle, 85, 87)
       (Deluxe Grade Two Barrel Rifle, 86, 87)
FARROW, E. S., *AMERICAN SMALL ARMS*, 175, 176.
FARROW, Milton, 84, 85
FLOBERTS, Belgian, 37, *38*, 39.
FOREST AND STREAM, 74.
FULLER, J. CUTLER, 100.

G

GARDNER, Robert, *SMALL ARMS MAKERS*, 74, 92, 95, 96.
GEBBY, Jeffy, 191, 195.
GEIGER, Leonard, 157.
GEIGER PATENT RIFLE, 156, *157*.
BRAND RAPIDS PUBLIC MUSEUM, 90, *91*.
GREENE RIFLE WORKS, 97.
GRIFFEN & HOWE WINCHESTER HIGH SIDE WALL, 195.
GUNN, G. P., 30.
GUN REPORT Magazine, 90.
GUNS Magazine, 14, 147.

K

KARNOPP, Kingsley, 14.
KERN, V., Nurnberg, 81.
KING, Nelson, 14.
KING NITRO, 44.
KIRKWOOD, David, 96.
   (Kirkwood Rifle, 96, 149.)
KITTEREDGE, B & COMPANY, 101.
KITTRELL, Bob, 47.
KLINKEL, Edson, 2, 8.
KNODE, O. M. "Jack", 14.
KOOZER, Ward, 197.

L

LANG, M. W., 78.
LEECH, Don, 51.
LEFEVER, Daniel M., 72, 73, 74, 92.
LEFEVER, Frank, 74.
LITTLE PAL, 40 (See TOWNLEY's)
LOVELL, Hervey, 181.
LYMAN GUN SIGHT CORPORATION, 199.
     (#210 Globe front sight, 18, 20.)
     (Side-of-Receiver sight, 20.)
     (#2A Windage,
     (Two Leaf rear sight, 2.)
     (Ivory Bead front sight, 2.)
     (Disc sight, 103.)
     (Folding Tang rear sight, 2, 17, 22.)
     (#17 Globe sight, 13.)
     (#6 sight, 16.)
     (#225107 bullet, 183.)
     (#225438 bullet, 183.)

M

MALCOLM TELESCOPIC SIGHT, 5, 96, 148, 153.
MANN, Dr. F. W., 173
    (*THE BULLET'S FLIGHT*, 175.)
MANN-NIEDNER firing pin, 189.
MARLIN FIREARMS COMPANY, 112, 113, 199.
MARLIN, J. M., 110, 111, 112.
MARTINI, 13, 14, 68, 69, 82, 98, 99.
   (Martini Cadet, 193.)
MASSACHUSETTS ARMS COMPANY, 150.
MAXIM SILENCER, 51.
MAYNARD, 6, 90, 109, 146, 148, 150, 151, 152, 185.
    (Number 14 Creedmoor, 148.)
    (Number 15 Model, 52, 183.)
    (Number 16 Model 1882, 149, 152.)
MC PHEETERS, John, 187, 189.
MEDICUS WOODCHUCK PRESERVE, 173.
MERIDEN FIREARMS COMPANY, 34.
    (Model 6, *34*.
    (Model 10, 34.)
MERRIMACK ARMS & MANUFACTURING COMPANY, 105, 107.
MILITARY MINIATURE RIFLES, 12.
MOGG, L. N., telescopic sight, 5.

210

(Stevens 404, 19, 181.)
(Stevens 044½, 21, 22, 185.)
(Stevens 45-44½, 22.)
(Stevens 52-44½, 22.)
(Stevens Model 110, 22, *23.*)
(Stevens Model 27, 24.)
(Stevens Scheutzen, 179.)